Inside
Commodity
Futures

Inside Commodity Futures

William D. Roszel, Ph. D.

Scott, Foresman and Company

Glenview, Illinois   London

This book is designed to provide accurate and authoritative information in regard to the subject covered. However, it is sold with the understanding that neither the author nor the publisher is engaged in rendering accounting, legal, tax, or other professional service. If expert assistance or legal advice is required, it is suggested that the reader seek the services of a competent professional person.

Library of Congress Cataloging-in-Publication Data

Roszel, William D.
  Inside commodity futures / William D. Roszel.
      p.   cm.
    1. Commodity futures.   I. Title
  HG6046.R67   1990
  332.63'28—dc20
                                                        89-24209
                                                            CIP

1 2 3 4 5 6 MPC 94 93 92 91 90 89

ISBN 0-673-46066-5

Scott, Foresman professional books are available for bulk sales at quantity discounts. For information, please contact Marketing Manager, Professional Books Group, Scott, Foresman and Company, 1900 East Lake Avenue. Glenview, IL 60025

CONTENTS

CONTENTS

INTRODUCTION

This should be your *first* book on commodities. Once you read it, you will know what the market is really all about. Then you can read trading manuals to get the nuts and bolts.

WHY THIS BOOK IS TIMELY

There are cycles in all investments. The late 1970s were the time to invest in real estate. It really didn't matter what real estate you invested in—everything quadrupled in value.

The 1980s were the time to invest in stocks. Again, it almost didn't matter which company you chose. As the DOW went from around 1,000 to over 2,500, almost any company did well and those who stuck their money in mutual funds, which played most of the companies, did particularly well.

The 1990s, I believe, are going to be the time of commodities. Commodities are where the quick and profitable action is going to be.

It won't be the first time. In 1974 and 1975 when the stock market dropped like a lead egg and when you couldn't give away a house, commodities were going crazy. Well, it's time again folks. Commodities in the 1990s are going to shine.

There are plenty of reasons for the emphasis on commodities, most of which we'll explore in the first part of this book. They include coming problems in agriculture, exacerbated by droughts, financial troubles for banks and saving and loans caused by non-performing loans in real estate and in the Third World, and the double debts of our trade deficit and national deficit. All of these make commodities look good. In fact, as the country and the economy get into increasingly serious trouble, commodities do better and better.

There is also a very strong chance that soon we will once again have high inflation, and commodities like nothing better than inflation.

INVESTMENT OF DISCONTENT

What's important to grasp here is that commodities do well when most other things do badly. If there's inflation coming, if there's a recession coming, most other investments are in trouble . . . but not commodities. In commodities you can make just as much money selling as you can buying.

That's why the troubled times of the 1990s are going to be perfect for commodities. That's why we've come full cycle once again.

DON'T MISS OUT

Remember that poor sap (I sincerely hope you don't see yourself here!) who bought into the stock market at 2,500 just before it crashed in October of 1987 saying to himself, "I can't stand it anymore. Everyone else but me is making money!"

Or that sad character who bought real estate at the peak in 1980 just before prices dropped saying to himself, "If only I had gotten in five years earlier. Think of all the money I've lost by sitting on the sidelines!"

The same thing is going to happen in commodities, mark my words. Those who get started early and learn how to invest in commodities are going to make their fortunes. Those who sit on the sidelines are still going to be there, lamenting their losses as we move into the next century.

Don't miss out. Commodities are THE investment for the 1990s. Be there!

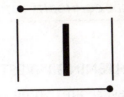

WHY YOU SHOULD INVEST IN COMMODITIES TODAY

There are only two kinds of people who should invest in commodities—those who are already rich . . . and those who want to become rich.

B. R.

I firmly believe that over the decade of the 1990s, commodities are going to be the hottest investment you will be able to find. If you're not there, if you're not taking advantage of the profits to be made, you're going to feel just like the poor soul who sat on the sidelines during the other great booms in recent history—the stock market of the mid-1900s, the silver boom during the late 1970s, or the real estate boom during the mid-1970s. You're going to watch others get rich—or richer—and there's no more sickening feeling than to see your friends making it while you miss out.

A FRIGHTENING INVESTMENT?

Many people, however, are going to stay away from commodities out of fear. The whole idea of commodities—the speed with which money can be made, or lost, the huge swings in capital—scares away many investors.

There's no denying that commodities are volatile (or that they offer enormous leverage)—that's actually their advantage. There's also no denying that you can lose your shirt in just a few minutes in commodities.

In the Chinese language the symbol for danger is the same symbol as for opportunity.

However, in this book I'm going to show you that commodities can be safe when viewed as part of an overall portfolio. I'm going to show you that through the use of a money manager you can reduce your risk to acceptable levels. I'm going to show you the inside story on commodities, that part of the field that only the insiders know . . . and as studies have shown, the insiders in commodities are getting amazingly rich.

WHAT ARE COMMODITIES?

Commodities are cattle, coffee, orange juice, soybeans, corn, plywood, silver, and other "commodities." They are the raw goods that farmers, miners, and others who work with natural resources produce. They are also financial instruments such as bonds, and they are currencies like deutsche marks and yen.

The important thing to remember is that to make money in commodities you don't have to be a farmer, rancher, miner, or banker. Can you even imagine coming home to your wife or husband one evening and saying, "Honey, I just invested $3,000 of our hard-earned money in pork bellies!"

The response is bound to be, "What in the world are pork bellies?"

To which I suspect 75 percent of commodity investors would have to reply, "I don't have the faintest idea! But they're going to make us rich."

The truth is that you don't have to have ever seen the commodity you invest in. You don't ever need to take possession of it or to hold it in your hands.

THE ROLE OF KNOWLEDGE AND INFORMATION

That's not to say, of course, that you don't need to have knowledge about commodities—knowledge and information are what make for success in commodity investing. But it's important to have a firm grasp on what kind of knowledge and what kind of information you really need. It's not the hands-on-the-plow kind, or the working-in-the-bank type.

Those who have dabbled in the commodities futures market know exactly what I'm talking about. Some of the most successful investors don't know a pork belly from a cocoa bean. But they know the market, they know themselves, and they know the people they hire to invest their money.

To seek advice means that one is well advised.

Roy Longstreet

That's what this book is about. It gets right down to the nitty-gritty of making money. Here's how those who get rich in commodities really do it.

Of course, you need to have some idea of how the market operates, and we'll get a taste of that in this chapter. (I've also prepared a brief appendix to give you more basic information—see Appendix 1.) But, here, now, you're going to get the essentials of what you need to know to make a profit. Certainly read all you can about commodities futures, about trading pits, about margin calls, about stop-loss orders, and all the rest. But, learn what you need to know to be successful here.

PROFIT FROM DIFFICULT TIMES

The fascinating thing about commodities is that you can make money regardless of which direction the price is moving. If corn is going up, you can make money all the way up. If copper is going down, you can make money all the way down. You can even go both ways so that as the price goes up in one commodity, silver for instance, and as the price goes down in another commodity, such as gold, you make money on the spread between them!

As long as there's volatility in the market, as long as there are price movements, you can make money. That's why commodities are said to be the investment of difficult times.

Consider, for example, natural disasters. Back in the summer of 1988, farmers in the midwest were experiencing the worst drought since the 1930s. There simply wasn't any rain for months and months. The crops were drying out and dying.

As a result of this, we were looking at a shortage of certain grains. At one point it looked as though fully a third to a half of the summer crop of soybeans would be destroyed. This meant opportunity for commodity traders.

Going Long

As commodity investors know, "going long" means that you enter into a contract in which you agree to buy a commodity at a specified time in the future for a price agreed to now. If the price goes up between now and the time you've agreed to buy, the difference is your profit. (Of course, in actual trading almost no one physically buys a commodity. Rather, sometime before the expiration of the contract—the date it's due—you execute an offsetting contract agreeing to sell a like amount of commodity. The difference between the two contracts is cash profit to you— or the loss if the trade went against you.)

In the summer of 1988, going long in grains was an excellent idea. The drought had produced shortages. Shortages meant higher prices. If you had opened a contract in January 1988 to go long in soybeans (to buy them, for example, six months in the future, to buy "June soybeans") you would have bought at a price of about $6 a bushel. (Remember, it's in January that you're entering into this contract. What you are agreeing to do is to pay $6 per bushel come June.)

Contracts are for set amounts of a commodity. In the case of soybeans, the contract is for 5,000 bushels. Since you're paying $6 for each bushel, the contract's value is $30,000. However, you don't have to put up the whole $30,000. Remember, you're only agreeing to buy in June.

SOYBEANS

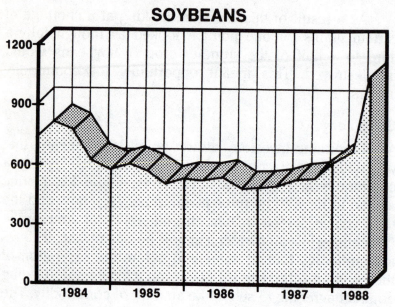

Five-year soybean prices.

Now it's January. All that you need to put up is a kind of guarantee that you'll honor your contract come June.

The guarantee is in the form of enough money to insure that if the price moves against you, if soybeans go down in value instead of up, you'll be able to meet your obligation. For example, if soybeans drop to $5.50 a bushel, your contract's value for 5,000 bushels has dropped to $27,500— a loss of $2,500. Therefore in soybeans you would be required to put up this amount of money, $2,500, in cash. This is called your "margin." (The actual cost of the trade— what you pay the broker—is minimal, typically under $100.)

So, you put up your margin of $2,500 (or $3,000 or whatever the minimum margin happens to be at the time) and you wait and hope. Then the drought hits, and soybeans go through the roof in price.

The Trade Is Successful

When June finally comes around, soybeans are selling for $10.50 a bushel. Simple arithmetic tells you if you subtract your contract price of $6.00 a bushel for the June value of soybeans of $10.50 a bushel, you can pocket the difference of $4.50 a bushel. Since the contract was for 5,000 bushels, that means you would have made $22,500! Your total investment would have been the establishment of that $2,500 margin back in January plus about $100 in fees for the trade. That's right, you invested $2,600 and you made $22,500. And that's on only one trade and one contract!

What's important to remember here is that you were making money off of hard times. The drought of '88 allowed you to profit.

Trading in the Summer of '88

I can remember that summer vividly. I had many open contracts, and I knew that the poor farmer was going down the tubes. Yet there I was on my knees every night saying, "Dear Lord, let it get dry because I'd like to buy a 31-foot yacht next year!" (I currently have a 28 footer—I buy a new boat every year.)

I was in the gallery watching the trading pits at the Board of Trade in Chicago during the summer of '88. On many days the trading in soybeans only lasted a few moments. As soon as trading tried to open, buyers pushed the price up until there was a "limit move" and trading was closed. (In certain trading months, contracts are only allowed to move a certain price limit each day. The idea is that this protects the unwary trader who gets caught in a big price move going against him. As we'll see later, limit moves usually harm you more than they help you.)

It was wonderful being long (buying) and watching the market move up the limit day after day. It was literally money in the pocket (since you can withdraw your profits each day from an open contract). The longer the drought held, the higher the price went, and if you held a long contract, every *penny* it moved up in soybeans was a profit of $50!

Of course, timing is critical to the market. In 1988, the price of soybeans depended, absolutely depended, on there being no rain. It was strictly a drought panic.

> *I never yet met a weatherman who could say for sure if it was going to rain next week.*
>
> B. R.

But anyone with common sense knows that it's got to rain sometime. So as soon as an upper price was established and those limit up moves ended and soybean contracts began to trade, anyone with savvy knew it was time to get out. If you were in the market and knew what you were doing, instead of continuing to hold onto your long contract hoping for the price to go forever higher, you offset it with a contract to sell and took your profit.

Going Short

Of course, if you were a real whiz kid at the market, you saw a new opportunity sitting there. You realized that what goes up must come down. That drought couldn't last forever and when it ended, prices would plummet. So, at the top of the market, you offered to short (sell) soybeans at the current price.

As commodity traders know, "going short" essentially means selling before you buy. It's a theoretical concept. If in January you can enter into a contract to buy soybeans in June with $30,000 (money that you don't have), why can't you in June enter into a contract to sell 5,000 bushels of soybeans (that you don't have) come next December?

Remember, in commodities there is almost never physical delivery. You're not required to come up with the soybeans, only to offset your contract. (You'll recall that "offsetting" means to enter into a contract to go in the other direction. In this case, offsetting means that sometime before your selling contract expires in December, you'll enter into a contract to buy which will offset it.)

Then the Rains Came

What happened next? Rain happened. It began to rain at the end of June. At first it was spotty, then a few cloudbursts and then . . . torrents. For a while it looked as though the entire crop was going to drown.

But soybeans are hearty, and though almost one-fourth of the crop was ruined by drought, three-fourths survived. That was enough, along with government soybeans in storage, to assure there would be no shortages. With no shortages, there was nothing to sustain the price.

Like a rock thrown off a tall building, prices plummeted. Just as a few weeks earlier there had been limit moves up each day, now we were faced with limit moves down. Those who were still long (buying) in soybeans were screaming that they were getting killed. But you had been smart. You sold at the top and went short (selling). In June you had entered into a contract to sell soybeans come December for a price of $10.50 a bushel.

Taking a Profit

You waited. By September, the price had fallen, because of the rains, so that soybeans were going for $8 a bushel. You decided not to push your luck. You traded out of soybeans with an offsetting contract (you entered into a contract to buy soybeans at $8 a bushel). Your contract to sell at $10.50 a bushel was now offset by your contract to buy at $8 a bushel and you pocketed the difference or $2.50 a bushel. On the 5,000 bushel contract that was another profit you just made of $12,500. Once again you had only put up the $2,500 margin plus about another $100 for the trade. You had made all of your money on less than $3,000 total investment!

THE LONG AND SHORT OF IT

Let's recap. You went long in January for $6.00. When the price went to $10.50 in June, you closed out your position pocketing $4.50 a bushel. Then you opened a new short position, agreeing to sell for $10.50. When the price dropped to $8 in September, you covered your position and pocketed the difference or $2.50 a bushel. (Don't be confused by "time" in commodity trading. Here as no where else in the world, you can sell before you buy!) Your total profit on the $3,000 investment was $34,500!

If you didn't quite follow the trades through this example, don't worry about it. You have plenty of time to learn the mechanics. (A further explanation is given in Appendix 1.) What's important to know is that you made money, lots of money, when the market was going up . . . and you made lots more money when the market was going down. Regardless of which direction the market was moving, if you were trading correctly, the profits were rolling in.

The other important thing is to understand that the profits were made by difficult times, in this case first drought, then torrential summer rains.

COMING HARD TIMES?

Commodities love hard times. Drought, as in the summer of 1988, is one aspect. More hard times are coming.

Most of us can recall that at the beginning of the 1980s there were those doomers and gloomers who were predicting that the economy would collapse, even that there'd be another world war. Well, I didn't believe it was going to happen and I certainly hope you didn't. Like a lot of other people, I invested in the future, in the stock market, and made a bundle.

Now, however, it's the beginning of the 1990s. Again there are the doomers and gloomers out there. But folks, I mean to tell you, this time I believed it . . . and you'd better believe it too!

The 1990s are going to be a watershed decade when we are going to see cataclysmic events happen to our lifestyle and our economy. (They may already have started happening by the time you read this.) In my opinion, we are going to see agricultural shortages, debt catastrophes, and banking collapses, all of which are going to lead to recession, inflation, and even possibly an incredible combination, recession and inflation combined.

It was the best of times. It was the worst of times.
Charles Dickens, *A Tale of Two Cities*

As bad as things get, however, it's going to be great for you, if you're into commodities. The reason is simple. Just as in our soybean example, the world around you may be going to pot, but you can make money as prices go up and as prices go down.

You'll be walking to the bank every day to deposit your profits. You'll be feeling terrible at the collapse that's occurring all around you. But every night before you go to bed, you'll be on your knees praying, "Dear Lord, let inflation get a point higher tomorrow" or, "Dear Lord, let the recession continue a few more months." Why? Simple, because next year you'll want to buy a 60-foot yacht!

In the next chapter I'm going to explain why I think we're set up for a big economic catastrophe and I'm going to show you how you can take advantage of it in commodities.

2

PROFITS FROM
DIFFICULT TIMES

Back in 1988 we had an election, and George Bush ran
against Michael Dukakis. Do you remember what the major
issues were? They were the pollution of Boston Harbor,
the pledge of allegience, and prison furloughs. This was
at the same time that Mexico and Brazil technically
defaulted on their loans to U.S. banks, that the Federal
Savings and Loan Insurance Corporation (which guarantees S&L deposits) went broke, and that our national deficit
approached three trillion dollars.

> *If you can't dazzle them with brilliance, baffle them with
> bullshit.*
>
> D. G.

The economic issues were screaming for attention,
yet both candidates skirted them. Why? It was because
neither candidate had any answers. The truth is, there are
no good answers to the problems we face.

The prosperity of the 1980s was built on borrowed
money. And that money will have to be paid back soon,

most likely in the 1990s. The process of paying for our past excesses is sure to be painful. Very likely it will involve a recession, inflation, unemployment, and more. Stocks, bonds, and real estate could get knocked flat on their backs during this period of time. Only commodities, which can be played when prices are going down as well as going up, are going to shine. In fact, to my way of thinking, the next decade offers a golden opportunity for those with the foresight to invest in commodities.

PAYING FOR THE 1980s

In order to understand what's likely to happen in the decade of the 1990s and how it provides a window of opportunity for commodities, it's necessary to first get a handle on where we are and where we came from. Yes, the problems the country faces are many, but which specific problems are going to create the investment opportunities of tomorrow?

> *"He's made greed into a national goal."*
> Newscaster describing Ronald Reagan in 1980

LIVING IN A DEBT ECONOMY

When you get down to it, there's really only one economic problem at the core of it all—debt. We owe so much that it's a burden. Others owe so much that they can't repay.

Those Who Owe Us

Third World countries, primarily those in South America, borrowed over $400 billion during the 1980s. They anticipated rapid growth fueled by high prices for their natural resources.

When oil prices collapsed, however, this plan was thrown out the window. Now these countries haven't a prayer of paying back what they owe. As of this writing, the banks (mostly American) that loaned them those funds, at the direction of the U.S. government, have loaned them additional funds with which to pay their interest. (It's like loaning your neighbor a hundred bucks at an interest rate of one dollar a month. At the end of the month, when he can't pay the dollar interest, you loan him another five. He pays you back one and you say your loan is producing interest. Would you be willing to do that for your neighbor? Interestingly enough, bankers are willing to do that for South American countries.)

Those We Owe

The American consumer (who has the lowest rate of savings of any consumer in any industrialized nation) has borrowed to the maximum in order to finance purchases of cars, clothes, perfumes, and millions of other goods many of which are imported from foreign countries.

As a result, we have a built-in trade deficit. That means we as Americans owe foreigners (the Japanese and Europeans) vast sums of money. Our trade deficit is currently running anywhere between $8 and $15 billion a *month*!

Of course, foreigners aren't all that stupid. They are wise to what we're doing, and each month they whittle away at us in the form of devaluing our currency. That translates into something like, "That French perfume,

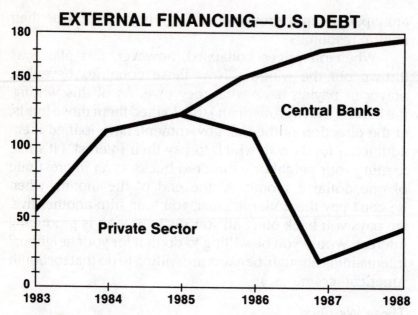

EXTERNAL FINANCING—U.S. DEBT

A dramatic increase in funding of U.S. debts from foreign private banks began after 1985.

madame, will cost you $200 today whereas it only cost you $150 last week."

The result of our trade imbalance is a falling dollar. Between 1982 and 1988 the dollar fell by 50 percent against the Japanese yen (from 240 yen to the dollar to roughly 120). During that same period, the dollar fell from 11 French francs to the dollar to 6. Similar falls have occurred against German, British, Swiss, even Italian currencies!

The dollar's decline (which I'll later discuss at length in terms of profiting from it through commodities futures) was caused by our insatiable appetite for borrowing. We can't afford it. But we want it anyway. So we borrow.

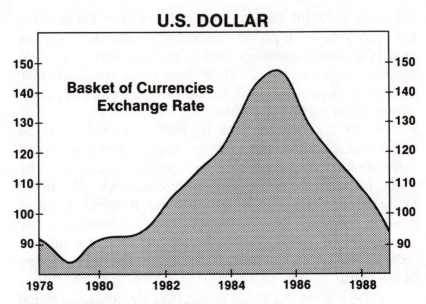

U.S. DOLLAR

Basket of Currencies Exchange Rate

The rise and fall of the U.S. dollar.

Our Biggest Debt

Of course, the biggest borrower of all is the federal government. When Ronald Reagan was President our federal debt soared to trillions of dollars. As of this writing, just the annual interest charge to service the accumulated national debt is currently running over $100 billion dollars. (If we didn't have the interest charge, we could probably balance the budget!)

Cutting taxes without cutting spending was like trying to fly a plane with only one wing.

Don't get me wrong. I'm not saying that Ronald Reagan was entirely to blame for this brewing catastrophe. He was definitely the right man for the job at the time. He restored the dignity and the power of the United States. His goals in supply-side economics were admirable and they could have been achieved . . . if he had been an economist. But Mr. Reagan never understood that you can't cut taxes without also cutting spending.

When he realized back in 1982 that he'd never be able to cut spending with a Democratic Congress, he should have abandoned supply-side economics. But instead, he opted for what he could get—a tax cut. It was like trying to fly an airplane with only one wing. It spiraled out of control, the result being ever increased borrowing to pay for continued spending. We ended up with the highest federal debt of any country at any time in the entire history of the world.

(The interesting thing is not that Mr. Reagan offered a flawed economic theory. Supply-side works when you cut spending as well as taxes. It's that Mr. Reagan offered half an economic theory. The miracle was that he was able to do it at all.)

To get the Reagan version of supply-side to work, we had to borrow huge sums of money to make up for the tax cuts. Back in '82 economists said the government could never borrow enough money to sustain the debt and keep the economy growing. They were a dime a dozen. I think they used to hang out on my street corner with signs reading, "It can't be done!"

But Mr. Reagan did it. He borrowed the money not just from Americans, but from Japanese, the Germans, and the other rich countries. We borrowed all we needed, getting the cream of it from foreigners who felt the U.S. was a safe haven (and because we have never defaulted on a debt in modern times).

Now we all owe all those people incredible fortunes. From being the greatest creditor nation in 1982, we went to being the biggest debtor nation the world has ever seen by 1989. (We owe far more to the other industrialized nations than the Third World owes to our banks!)

WHERE DO WE GO FROM HERE?

Of course, that's all just preamble to the opportunities of the 1990s. It's ancient history.

Today:

1. Third World countries are threatening to destroy our banking system with their inability to pay back their debt.
2. Insolvent savings and loans are shutting down across the country as Congress and the White House struggle to bail them out without causing panic.
3. Consumers are running out of credit with which to borrow ever more.
4. The dollar is bouncing all over the place.
5. The federal deficit is out of control.
6. Foreigners are beginning to wonder how long they can continue to lend us money before we (like Third World countries) can no longer pay.

Where will it all end? What's ultimately going to happen?

My feeling is that Ronald Reagan, as President, was a kind of magician. He kept the illusion alive, and he kept the whole incredible economic mess from falling apart. We aren't likely to get many more magicians. Certainly George Bush isn't proving to be one. In the 1990s we are likely to see the bottom drop out of everything.

A DIFFERENT KIND OF RECESSION?

Here's the most likely scenario. First, we are going to get a recession. The economic expansion of the 1980s was the longest in history. It has to end sometime, and when it does (perhaps it already has as you read this), we would normally expect a recession. The coming recession, however, is going to be unlike any other you've ever experienced.

Those who don't learn from the past are condemned to an even more vile future.

B. R.

In addition to the usual slowdowns which occur during any recession—cutbacks on consumer spending, slow or no growth in industry, unemployment, and lower wages—the next recession may have some additional and decidedly nasty features.

Higher Interest during Recession?

Remember, a recession means that everyone in general is earning less money. Hence, the government takes in lower revenues through taxes. That means that in order to keep spending at current levels, the government *has to borrow more.* During the next recession, the annual budget deficit will swell enormously.

In addition, to help the country pull out of the recession, the government is likely to even *increase* spending. (This is the standard remedy for recessions popularized by Sir John Maynard Keynes during the Great Depression of the 1930s—governments need to spend more money during recessions in order to put people back to work and bail the country out.)

If the government spends more, the deficit will rise even more. Some economists are pointing to incredible deficits in the 1990s during the next recession of from $300 to $500 billion *a year*!

Where is that money going to come from? Certainly not from Americans. As I noted, we're the worst savers in the world. We simply don't have any money to lend Uncle Sam. The government once again has to try to borrow that money from abroad.

But will we be able to get it this time? Will the Japanese and Germans and other foreigners be willing to lend the world's largest debtor nation hundreds of billions of dollars during a recession? C'mon, folks, even foreign bankers are not that stupid!

Some day, some place in the government, a Japanese or German banker is going to suddenly pick up his portfolio and walk out of a meeting room and the word, "No!" is going to reverberate through the halls of the U.S. Treasury.

Short-term solutions will surely follow. There will be a hue and cry to increase interest rates. Higher interest rates *always* attract money.

But, what will raising interest rates do if it is done in the middle of a recession? It will make borrowing even more difficult for American consumers. History has shown that raising interest rates during a recession deepens and lengthens that recession. Hiking interest rates is a band-aid. But it ultimately results in making the wound fester and become more diseased.

Inflation during Recession

At some point, someone in the Federal Reserve bank (our equivalent of a national bank) is going to see that raising interest rates is not the answer. That person in authority is going to see that hiking interest rates deepens the recession and reduces revenues from taxes, requiring ever more borrowing, resulting in ever higher interest rates to attract money—a vicious cycle that can only end in the deepest depression the country has ever seen.

> *Stopping inflation is like trying to stop after you've eaten one potato chip.*
>
> B. R.

When that official sees this, he or she is going to desperately look for another solution.

What is the only other solution available? Inflate our currency. Pay back our huge deficit, yes, dollar for dollar, but with new dollars worth only ten cents as much as the dollars that were borrowed.

Mark my words. Just as inflation was seen as the bogeyman at the end of the 1970s, it is going to be seen as the solution (by the federal government) in the 1990s. We could have inflation like we've never had before.

LEARNING FROM BRAZIL

You don't think it can happen? Think again. Consider the case of Brazil. In 1986, that country, heavily burdened by debt it borrowed from foreigners, mainly American bankers, put itself on an austerity plan. It sought to reduce government expenses by cutting federal jobs and wages. It worked hard to reduce imports and build an industrial base. For a time it looked like the plan was going to work. The inflation rate in Brazil, which had been an incredible 300 percent annually, dropped to under 100 percent by 1987. The need for borrowing was reduced. Just a few more years of austerity and the Brazilian government would turn the country around, economically speaking.

Then a new administration came in. Federal workers struck in protest at layoffs and reduced wages. Whole industries were shut down. The leftists began signing up people in droves, panicking the government.

The new government desperately came to the World Bank and the U.S. seeking new loans. Some were given, a few billion dollars, peanuts in this ball game. Things only got worse. Then the military threatened to revolt or to quit en masse.

No man and no country can endure pain forever.

E. Soares

The government gave in. It stopped cutting jobs. It increased wages, in some cases by an immediate 50 percent! The finance minister came to the president in a rage demanding to know where he was to get the money to pay for all the new and generous decrees. No one would loan Brazil another dime.

"From cruzeros," was the answer he was given. Cruzeros, the currency of Brazil was to provide the answer. Just print more, as many as were needed.

It was done. Millions, billions, trillions of cruzeros were printed. The result, of course, was inflation . . . massive inflation.

By the end of 1988, the inflation rate in Brazil had skyrocketed from 100 percent to 1200 percent! As soon as people would get their paycheck, they would run to buy something . . . anything! If they waited, even a single day, the value of their paycheck could drop by 5 percent! If they waited a week, they could lose a third of their buying power . . . wait a month and they would be wiped out.

As of this writing there is talk of hyperinflation in Brazil of the kind Germany saw after World War I. It could take a million cruzeros to buy a loaf of bread. The complete collapse of the country could follow.

Remember, Brazil is the eighth largest economic power in the world.

IT CAN'T HAPPEN HERE

Brazil's problems could actually trigger a collapse in this country. Remember, Brazil owes U.S. bankers in excess of $100 billion. If it can't, or won't, pay, those bankers are in very big trouble. For some of them, the amount owed is greater than their total capitalization! (When you lose more than you're worth, it's called insolvency.)

Further, there are some disturbing similarities. Brazil is a debtor nation. But so is the U.S. While Brazil owes us, we owe Japan, Germany, and other European countries. If Brazil defaults, those who lend us money are going to think twice about it. *There is every indication that if during a recession we need to borrow $300 to $500 billion to make up our budget deficit, we won't be able to find lenders.*

Never say never.

B. R.

Hyperinflation could happen here. In some ways we're more set up to produce inflation than Brazil was. (If you still think it can't happen, read the next chapter).

PROFITS

However as the song says, look for the silver lining. The world's falling apart all around you, but you're living like a prince in a castle. How? By investing in commodities.

Remember, inflation adds volatility to the commodities market, and volatility is like the jingle of a cash register. Inflation at the same time as recession (should it occur) just means a bigger cash register.

It's going to be like the stock market in early 1987. It didn't matter what you bought—everything was going up! Come the next economic catastrophe, stocks probably won't be worth the paper they're written on. But commodities, that's where the action is going to be. That's where the profits are going to be found. The dollar goes down—buy yen. Silver goes up—buy silver. Government securities go down—sell them.

As we'll see in subsequent chapters, the opportunities are endless. But first, a few more details on inflation.

3

THE COMING
INFLATION?

This is a true story I tell at my seminars. We used to have a Cadillac that we used to pick up clients and bring them to the office. It was a leased car, and the lease was costing us around $400 a month.

The Cadillac was top of the line, almost a chauffeur model. At the end of the three years, it was time to turn it in and get another one. I sent one of my employees to the car dealer to handle the details. He phoned me back and told me that for the same model car, the lease would be $700 a month. It was almost a doubling of cost.

I exploded, but then I saw a lesson there. The value of that car had inflated more than 75 percent in three years. Now I ask you, where in that story do you see the 4 percent inflation that the government has been talking about for the past few years?

I don't know how it's done or where the mirrors are hidden—maybe they upgrade one car model and downgrade another—but I can tell you for certain that it costs you a heck of a lot more to buy a car this year than it did last year.

I'm not saying that inflation is going to come back in and catch everyone's attention. I don't know if the government statistics are ever going to show an inflation rate over 4 or 5 percent. I'm just saying that if you go to buy anything, you're going to quickly realize that inflation is here.

Inflation is like smog—it's when you can't see it that it's really killing you.

B. R.

It's not just Cadillacs . . . it's everything. I believe that the only difference between this inflationary period and the last is the public's perception. Thus far, the vast majority of people still want to believe the government statistics. Thus far, people want to believe that inflation is only 4 or 5 percent.

THE PIZZA INFLATION RATE

I have some friends at Manufacturer's Hanover Bank who say they've done a study of the real rate of inflation. Never mind what the government says inflation is in the Consumer Price Index and the Wholesale Price Index. The real rate of inflation, according to these people, was closer to 12.5 percent in 1988 and higher in 1989.

I call the real rate of inflation the pizza rate. Go out and buy a pizza and see how much more it costs you today than it did last month or last year. Now you're looking real inflation in the face. Try it on clothes or food or anything that you buy. Haven't you seen the price increases?

"But," many well-meaning and innocent people ask, "how can that be? How can the government statistics be so far wrong?"

Part of the answer, plain and simple, is manipulation. The government keeps switching the components of the inflation indices to reflect the lowest possible rates. Did you know, for example, that the government reduced the importance of the price of purchasing a house as a major component of the Consumer Price Index? Why? Because a few years ago it was raising the index "too fast and too high." Thus, it could no longer be considered "reliable." Instead rental costs are currently weighed heavier as a major component. Why? Because rental costs haven't risen nearly as much in recent years.

But let rental rates rise and you can be darned sure they'll be downgraded in the CPI. The truth is, anything that makes the Consumer Price Index rise is considered suspect. If it makes it rise too much, it's removed or downgraded in consideration. Is it any wonder that the government keeps boasting about low inflation?

INFLATION AND WAGES

Besides switching around the components, the other way in which the government keeps the CPI and WPI down is through wage restraint. Forty-four percent of the Consumer Price Index is the wage component . . . nearly half. As long as wages don't go up across the board, you're not going to see much inflation reflected in the Price Index. Cadillacs and bread may go up 10 percent, but if wages only go up 1 or 2 percent, the index as a whole is going to remain fairly stable.

In the past, as soon as the cost of goods went up, workers demanded and received higher wages. Thus, in years past the CPI took big jumps.

Today, however, you won't see wages go up, no matter how much the prices of other items go up. The reason is that Mr. Reagan, when he was in office, in effect killed the unions in this country.

When Reagan broke the airline controllers' union back at the beginning of his first term in 1980, it was a clear signal to every employed person in this country. That signal said, "You ask for higher wages, we'll fire you and find somebody to do the job for half of what we're currently paying you!"

It happened with the tug boat workers in New York Harbor and with the auto workers in Detroit. The thinking of both union and non-union workers in this country changed. From, "Let me keep up with the cost of living," it turned into, "Let me keep up with my mortgage payments."

Back in the 1970s, the cry was for higher wages to keep up with inflation. When have you heard that cry recently? Teachers' unions are thrilled to get a 2 or 3 percent raise. If we believe the government's figures of 5 percent inflation, that means that those teachers are actually receiving a 2 percent reduction in salary! If we believe the Pizza rate, they're receiving about a 10 percent cut in salary . . . and they're thrilled! Do you know why? It's because they're still hanging on to their jobs.

INFLATION AS PERCEPTION

Do remember that old Hans Christian Andersen tale about the emperor who had no clothes? The emperor would go out in public stark naked and ask everyone what they thought of his new clothes. Since he was the emperor, with the right to chop off their heads if he didn't like their answer, it was to the populace's distinct advantage to believe the emperor was really wearing fine new clothes . . . and they told him so day after day after day.

The same thing is happening today. As long as workers are more concerned about keeping their jobs than about keeping up with real earning power, they are going to choose to perceive that there is little or no inflation. And as long as they do that, the 44 percent of the CPI that represents wages isn't going to budge, and the government is going to continue to smugly say that inflation isn't a threat in this country.

But what if one child should shout out, "Why, the emperor has no clothes . . . !"

THE PRESSURE OF FULL EMPLOYMENT

It almost happened in mid-1989. Employment had steadily been rising until the unemployment rate was dipping close to 5 percent. You could see it everywhere you looked. Every fast food restaurant had a sign up that read, "Help Wanted." It became so difficult to find certain types of employees that in the State of Massachusetts "headhunters" were going to the South and offering free transportation and initial room and board to anyone who would go up North and take a job.

The pressure of too few workers threatened for a time to cause employees to look around and reevaluate their wages. The average worker began to wonder and for the first time in nearly a decade began to say, "Hey, if they can't find enough people to work, maybe I should be getting more money for my job."

Workers almost saw that the emperor had no clothes. They almost saw that what they were losing to inflation. Except . . . there were all those homeless people out on the streets.

Remember the vast army of homeless in America? Never mind that many of them are the mentally ill, turned out of closed mental institutions, or that many others are totally unskilled and incapable of finding labor in a high-tech society. Just the fact that they are out there is enough to keep American workers holding their tongues. You want to argue for higher wages, look out the window and see some poor individual sleeping on a grating. That'll put the fear into you. That'll keep you believing that the emperor really is wearing clothes.

One of the cleverest, though certainly the most heartless, moves that Reagan made while in office may have been to close the mental hospitals and the shelters for the poor and thus create that army of homeless. Just seeing them on the streets has been enough to keep the American worker in line.

Don't get me wrong. I'm not saying that we should be paying workers anything more in wages. The more any given worker produces for the same wages, the greater his productivity. One way for America to work itself out of the economic bind it's in, in the long run, is to become more productive. If we become an army of fast-working, low-paid zombies, we could conceivably outproduce even the Asian countries and regain our status of world economic superiority.

Only that's not for me . . . and I trust that's not for you either.

INFLATION AS A WINDOW OF OPPORTUNITY

What my goal is . . . and what I believe your goal should be . . . is to understand the economic realities of the 1990s and to profit from them.

We are entering a period of time when we can expect to see something quite unprecedented. We may see a combination of recession, high interest rates, and even high inflation—all at the same time! (If we're perceptive, we can see it happening right now all around us.)

I've made more money during inflation than during any other economic period.

B. R.

However, if we're average people, we're going to just sit back and let it wash over us, eating away whatever capital we've accumulated. We'll continue with the tried and true, we'll continue thinking the emperor is wearing clothes . . . and we'll get financially killed!

On the other hand, if we're creative, we'll see the 1990s not as a time of collapse, but as a window of opportunity.

Do you remember back in 1974 and 1975? Investment advisors were predicting a boom market in stocks. Only a recession hit and the stock market dropped 40 percent in value. If you were in traditional investments at that time, you lost your shirt.

On the other hand, during that same period, the commodities market almost doubled in value. Those who were trading commodity futures were sitting on top of the world. Personally, I was making into the mid six figures in commodities at that time.

Well folks, I'm here to tell you it's going to happen again. It's not going to be exactly the same, of course. Stocks are going to continue to be viable for quite some time. But the real money, the real profits, are going to be made in commodities. The window of opportunity is open for commodities. They are where the real profits are going to be found.

INFLATION OR NO INFLATION?

I personally think that inflation is here now, that it's getting worse, and that it's only a matter of time until the rest of you wake up and realize it. But I could be wrong. There might be no inflation.

That's the beauty of commodity investing. Yes, commodities love inflation and you can make an easy fortune there during inflationary times. But you can also make a fortune in commodities even if there's no inflation! Just let us go into a deflationary recession, and you'll see the commodity markets sparkle.

The truth is that it doesn't matter! Commodities are the opportunity of the decade. Hurray for them if inflation is here. But hurray for them anyway. If you're not into commodities soon, inflation or no, you're going to lose out on the opportunity of the decade.

4

LEVERAGE, LIQUIDITY, AND SAFETY IN COMMODITIES

The most quoted study in all commodities is one that was done in the early 1970s by the Coffee, Sugar and Cocoa Exchange in New York. That study said that of *all* the people who traded commodity futures, fully 85 percent lost *all* of the money they invested. Only 15 percent made money.

You can prove anything with statistics.
President Dwight D. Eisenhower

That study has been quoted a thousand times by those who advocate other investments—from mink farms to pearl diving—as *proof* that commodity investing is dangerous, risky, and no place for any but the most daring investors. The misunderstandings caused by that study have done more to keep investors away from commodity futures than anything else.

You see, what that study really said was that 85 percent of all *first year* traders lose money trading commodities. But of those traders who lasted into the second year, 70 percent made money. Now that's a horse of a different color.

What the study really showed was not that commodity trading was inherently a losing investment. It showed that commodity trading has a very steep learning curve. Once you master that curve, your chances of profiting were probably higher than in most other investment fields.

THE LEARNING CURVE OF COMMODITIES

If you have a probability of 85 percent of losing money in the first year and 70 percent of making money in the second year, what's the difference? What did you learn between year one and year two?

It's when you think you know it all that your troubles really begin.

B. R.

The answer, I believe, is that if you were one of the successful investors, sometime after the third or fourth month of trading, you fired your broker and ended up trading yourself. Or you fired your broker and hired a professional money manager. Either way, you stopped making your broker rich and learned enough about commodities to make yourself rich.

THE TROUBLE WITH COMMODITY BROKERS

I can still remember when I first became a commodities broker. I moved across the aisle from stocks and bonds to commodities and suddenly everyone was snickering. What were they snickering about?

It was because, to those in the business, a commodity broker is considered to have "terminal financial cancer." It's not a matter of "if" he will draw down his accounts and lose everybody's money . . . but "when." Of course, at the time I didn't know any better, so I went into commodities and immediately made everybody, including myself, rich.

You see, the thing about most commodities brokers is that they are always trading and looking for new clients. Let's go back to that study I mentioned at the beginning of this chapter. It also noted that at the time, and this was in the early 1970s, the average broker had 20 accounts and $60,000 under management. Off of this, the average broker was making $25,000 a year.

Now those figures may not seem remarkable until you realize that commission generation is generally one-third of trading fees. In order for that broker to get $25,000 for himself, he had to generate $75,000 in commissions for his house. He had to generate $75,000 in commissions on $60,000 under management.

Is it any wonder that 85 percent of those entering the market in the first year lost money? If they doubled their money, they were just standing still because they were paying so much in commissions.

The culprit and the reason so many lose so much in the first year of trading is not commodities . . . it's the broker.

If there are mediocre doctors, lawyers, and accountants, why should there not be mediocre brokers?

B. R.

That infamous study also went on to say that the average life of a commodities account was only four months. That meant that John Q. Public came in, opened an account for $3,000, lost the $3,000 in three or four months and was gone swearing to everyone that he or she met that commodities was too risky.

CHURNING

But don't you see, it wasn't the commodities that did these people in. It was the system. Brokers were driven to churn those accounts in order to make those commissions. Commissions in commodities are cheap. The average commission is about $75 for a "round trip" (trading in and then trading out). Do you have any idea how many trades a broker has to make to run his commissions up to $75,000 when each one is just $75? It's a thousand trades in and out. If the average broker had only twenty accounts, he had to move those twenty accounts 50 times a year. With all that trading, is it any wonder that brokers make money and accounts lose money?

What should a commodity broker be doing with his or her time? The obvious answer is that he or she should be studying the market so that the broker can tell you when to make those two or three good trades that come each year that can make you money. (We'll have much more to say about picking the right trades in a later chapter.)

But what do commodity brokers really do? If that study was accurate (I think it was) and the average account only lasts four months, they are constantly on the phone trying to solicit new accounts. And as soon as they get the new accounts, they are busy trading them in and out so they can make their commissions.

COMMODITIES AND GAMBLING

My goal in this chapter is not to knock commodity brokers, though many of them should be knocked, but instead to demonstrate why commodity futures have gotten a bad name and to show you how you can make money with reasonable safety in the market. First, you have to understand the pitfalls, the biggest of which we've just covered . . . the time it takes you to learn that your broker is interested more in commissions than your profits. In a later chapter we'll go into how to find a money manager who will be on your side.

The second reason commodities have gotten a bad name is that many people say and believe that commodities investing is just another form of gambling. I have heard it said more than once, "If you're thinking about investing in commodities, you might as well go to Las Vegas and lose your money on the gambling tables. You've got a better chance at the casinos than at the futures market!" Many people consider commodities nothing more than legalized and formalized gambling. Those people just don't know what they're talking about.

I can, however, understand their perspective. Superficially, it seems that there are a lot of similarities between gambling and commodities. Trading can be viewed as a wager, margins can be seen as gambling money, and risk can be viewed as luck.

We all make our own luck.

Bernard Baruch

However, upon closer scrutiny the similarities diminish. Commodities are no more gambling than buying stock, bonds, or real estate. In some way they are much less so.

Commodities are a zero sum game, gambling is not. In commodities if you have a loser, you have to have a winner. For those 85 percent of the people who lost all their money, there was the 70 percent of the second year traders who were making it.

To put it differently, in Las Vegas there are the house odds which always give the house a substantial advantage against you. In commodities there are no house odds, no advantage against you. If the odds were exactly even on every single gambling table in a casino, you would see the house go broke on a regular basis. Why? Simple— they would lose half the time. In commodities, the odds are even, and if you have any knowledge of how to speculate in the market at all, you should be able to win half the time.

In addition, in casinos you can't play a money management system. The casinos hate system players, particularly counters. Why? Because those people reduce the house's odds until it's close to even, and the house doesn't want that. A guy who really knows what he's doing in terms of counting and money management could go in there and clean them out.

In Las Vegas or Atlantic City, there's no rule against your losing money. But if you have a system that allows you to make money, that's against the rules.

In commodities, on the other hand, not only can you have a system, but you can have a computerized system. Today, savvy commodities investors trade in and out of the market on the basis of computer models that give them the edge over players who don't have such systems. In other words, in commodities you can actually turn the edge in your favor!

To summarize, in commodities

1. There are no house rules (other than the fairness rules of the Commodities Trading Commission and the Commodity Exchanges).
2. There is no house edge. The commodities exchanges do not take any part of your profits.
3. There is no rule against your having or using a system, even a computerized trading system.

You start out with the odds being exactly even. Then, if you develop a computerized money management system (described in the later chapters), you can actually put the odds in your favor. In gambling you start out with the odds against you. If by careful study and the use of money management and counting systems, you reverse some of the games so that the odds are at least even, you are thrown out!

Therefore, I think it's reasonable to say that comparing commodities to gambling really isn't appropriate. Your chances of success in commodities are far greater—or chances of losing—on the whole, are far less than with gambling. But does that say that commodities are a *safe* investment?

COMMODITIES AND SAFETY

Let me preface any comments on safety by pointing out that according to the study I quoted earlier, 85 percent of those who invest in commodities in the first year lose all their money. *You can lose quickly and heavily in commodities.*

Figure that you're going to lose a good percent of the time. It's going to happen no matter what. That way when it happens, you won't feel so bad.

B. R.

Having said that, let me go on to point out that as part of an overall portfolio, commodities can be considered to be a safe investment, as we'll see shortly. To see how, let's first consider the two elements of commodities that those who don't understand the field think are the main causes of risk—liquidity and leverage. (Actually they are what contribute to the field's safety!)

LEVERAGE

The leverage that you get with commodities is higher than in almost any other investment medium. A typical margin requirement is $3,000. (The margin will vary according to the commodity, the exchange's rules, and the house's requirements. I'll have more to say about margins later.) For that $3,000 you may control 5,000 ounces of silver, 120,000 pounds of rice, 30,000 pounds of fresh broiler chickens, or 100 ounces of gold. Let's take gold as our example since it has a smaller, and hence easier to deal with, quantity—100 ounces. If gold is selling for $400 an ounce and you control 100 ounces, that means that you control $40,000 worth of gold, for a $3,000 margin. Your leverage is roughly 11 to 1.

In most commodities the leverage is in the 10 to 1 or greater range. Consider what that means to you. In the

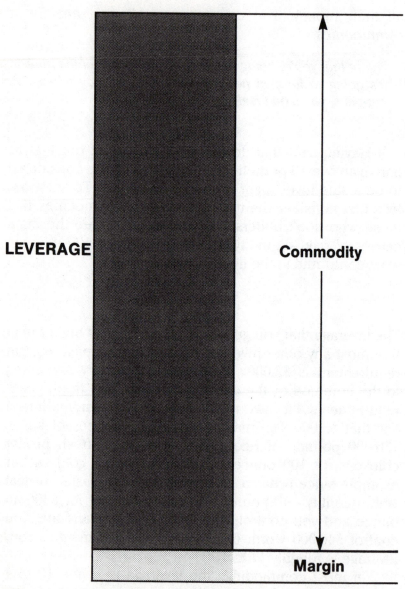

Leverage—the relationship of margin to value of commodity.

case of gold, if the price goes up just $3 an ounce, you make $300. (Remember, you control 100 ounces.) If the price goes down $3 an ounce, you lose $300.

A mere $3 an ounce fluctuation on the price of the commodity can result in a $300 (or 10 percent) gain or loss on your total $3,000 investment.

Another way to think of it is as a pyramid. The small end of the pyramid is your initial margin investment. The large end is the commodity you control.

A Word about Margins

It's important to understand that the money you initially put up does *not buy* the commodity. Rather you open a *contract* with the commodity exchange through a brokerage house in which *you agree to buy, or sell, a commodity at a specific future date for a specific price*. The margin is a deposit to guarantee your performance under the contract.

If the commodity moves in the direction you bought (for example, you were long and the commodity goes up in price) the *profit* you realize is immediately entered into your account and you may withdraw it.

If the commodity moves against you, the loss is deducted from your margin. If it continues to move against you and your margin is drawn down below what the commodity exchange and your brokerage house consider prudent levels to ensure your obligation under the account, you may be required to reinstate the margin to the original level. (You get a margin call.) Usually the brokerage house maintains a maintenance account that is used to replace the margin account. (If you put up $3,000, typically half or $1,500 is margin and half is maintenance.)

The market is always right . . . even when it's wrong.

Jesse Livermore

As noted above, you can get a "margin call" which is a demand to replace. If you fail to come up with the money, the brokerage house may trade you out of the commodity, giving you an immediate loss. If you come up with the margin call, the house will continue to keep your trade open.

See Appendix 1 and later chapters for more information on margin calls and "maintenance calls."

Profits from Leverage

It is the 10 to 1 or greater leverage that allows you to make the huge profits possible in commodity futures.

If you're still not sure of how leverage works, here's an analogy that I give in my seminars that should clear up any residual confusion. It's a comparison of commodities with real estate.

Let's say you buy a beautiful single-family home on a large lot for $100,000. (I realize the price is low for today's market, but let's not worry about that. The even figure makes it easier to understand the example and besides, we're concerned with commodities here, not real estate!)

You put 10 percent down ($10,000).

Now, let's say that after a year the market has gone up 10 percent. The house you bought for $100,000 is now worth $110,000. What percentage of profit, on paper, have you made?

If you answered 10 percent, I'm sorry, but you're wrong. You made 100 percent in profit *on paper*. Remember, you only invested $10,000. If your investment goes up by $10,000, that's twice the money invested or a 100 percent profit.

It's all possible due to leverage.

Of course, in real estate, it's frequently only on paper. You can't really get the profit out. The commission (typically 6 percent) and the closing costs (typically 5 percent) would eat up your profit. If your house only went up $10,000, it would probably cost you $11,000 to sell it, giving you a net loss of $1,000 on your investment.

LIQUIDITY

Costs of sale aside (remember, a commodities trade, in and out, is only about $75!), there's another and far more significant problem with real estate—liquidity. As anyone who has ever invested in property can testify, sometimes the market is hot . . . and sometimes it's cold. And when the real estate market is cold, you can't sell your property even if you give it away.

The truth about real estate is that it's illiquid. You often can't get your cash out when you want to. That's why honest real estate brokers always tell you to consider real estate a long-term investment—three to ten years. You may hit a slump or cold period and not be able to sell your property. (Don't make the ridiculous mistake of thinking that real estate never goes down or never slumps. Talk to the farmers in the Midwest or the people in the oil-patch states of Texas and Oklahoma—they'll tell you a few things about real estate slumps!)

I always know what side of the bread the butter's on.
                                                    W. C. Fields

You may stick your $10,000 in real estate and see it double due to leverage. Only, because of the market, you may not be able to sell for years! By then, your profit could dwindle, and because you didn't have the cash, you couldn't take advantage of other investments. (Some real estate brokers say you can always borrow against your property to get your money out. The trouble with that is you end up with higher payments which you usually have to make with money out of your pocket. That's hardly what I call getting your money out!)

On the other hand, consider a commodities investment. What if you could get the same leverage possible in real estate, only you could get your money out any time you wanted it? What if you could call up on the phone and say, "I'm up 100 percent, trade me out," and by the time you put down the phone, the trade had been completed? What if even before you traded out you could call up your broker and say, "I'm up 100 percent, send me a check for that amount and keep my position open!"?

Do you see the difference? Commodities not only offer the leverage that you can find in real estate, but they offer more. They offer liquidity.

SAFETY

Now that we've covered leverage and liquidity, let's get to that bugaboo that scares most people off . . . safety. Are commodities safe or not?

Obviously, if you're in that 85 percent who lose all their money in the first year of trading, they're not safe. On the other hand, if you're in that 70 percent who make money in their second year of trading, they are. The truth is somewhere in between.

Probably the best way to understand commodity safety is in terms of a study done by John Lintner of Harvard University a few years ago. Dr. Lintner compared the effect of investing in a portfolio of half stocks and half bonds with a portfolio of 40 percent stocks, 40 percent bonds, and 20 percent commodities. The results of the study astonished not only him, but the investment community as well. (See Appendix 2 for more on the Lintner study.)

The difference between an amateur and a professional is that the professional only makes a mistake once.

B. R.

The portfolio where commodities were combined with stocks and bonds did better in every case than the portfolio of just stocks and bonds alone. In other words, those who invested 20 percent of their portfolio in commodities were safer, meaning that there was less risk of loss, than a person who bought stocks and bonds alone.

How could that be? How could an investment as volatile as commodities, where prices jump up and down every day, add safety to an overall portfolio?

The answer has to do with leverage, liquidity, and a new factor, negative correlation.

NEGATIVE CORRELATION

What Dr. Lintner and numerous other investors and brokers have found is that when stocks and bonds (and real estate and many other investments) fall out of bed, commodities are soaring. And when stocks and bonds (and other investments) are doing very well, commodities tend to stagnate. That's called negative correlation.

The best example we have of that was during the 1974 and 1975 recession, one of the deepest the country has seen. During that recession, stocks and bonds were off 40 percent. Investors who put their money in those markets lost their shirts. At the same time, commodities across the board were up hundreds of percent. Those who invested there looked like financial geniuses.

Another way to think of a negative correlation is as a playground seesaw or teeter-totter. When stocks and bonds (and other investments) are up, commodities are down and vice versa.

(This only confirms what was said in the earlier chapters of this book, namely that commodities perform well during difficult economic times. During recession and particularly during inflation, the stock and bond markets go to pieces. But during those same periods is when commodities shine.)

COMBINING NEGATIVE CORRELATION
WITH LEVERAGE AND LIQUIDITY

The reason Dr. Lintner's study demonstrated that the negatively correlated commodities would offset losses in stocks and bonds to provide better overall safety in a portfolio has to do with leverage and liquidity.

The money that an investor lost in the 80 percent of his portfolio of stocks and bonds when the market turned down, was more than made up by the 20 percent he had invested in commodities because of the 10 to 1 or greater leverage in commodities. It only takes a 20 percent of a portfolio in commodities to offset an 80 percent investment in stocks and bonds because in the latter, you have either no leverage or at best 2 to 1 leverage (if you borrow on margin to buy your stocks). With commodities, however, your leverage is better than 10 to 1.

Further, with commodities, you can get your profits out immediately while maintaining your position. Thus, as you lose on stocks and bonds in a recession or other down period, you can withdraw funds from commodities profits to compensate on a daily basis, if needed.

> *You must be part scientist, part mathematician, and part artist to be successful in commodities. None have to be big parts.*
>
> B. R.

Dr. Lintner's conclusion was that by including commodities as a part of an overall portfolio, the investor could reduce the risk of volatility. That is, he could reduce his losses.

MODERN PORTFOLIO THEORY (MPT)

I have built on the work of Dr. Lintner and have modified his theories to come up with my own investment model which I call Modern Portfolio Theory or MPT.

The basic question I raise is, if commodities help to balance volatility in an overall portfolio, why couldn't an investor hone in on just the profits that the commodities offer? In other words, why use commodities just to balance out losses on stocks and bonds? Why not use commodities to make profits on their own?

Another way to think of this is the sawtooth pattern of investing. A typical investment portfolio over A period of time has this sawtooth appearance.

Dr. Lintner's study showed how to mitigate the effects of the sawtooth. He showed how to reduce the volatility so that lows of the sawtooth weren't as low. My theories suggest that we can use a similar approach to cut off the lows entirely and just keep the highs.

The key to doing this, of course, is to be able to invest in commodities during those periods when they will do

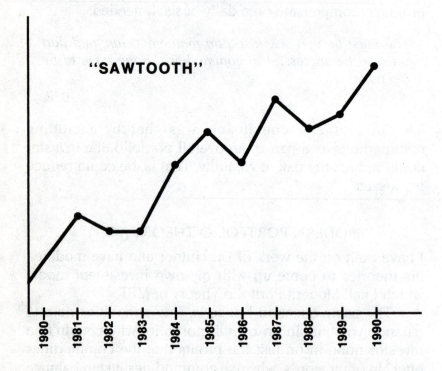

The "sawtooth" appearance of a typical investment. (Few high-profit investments show steady profit or loss.)

well and to stay out of the market when commodities are flat and stocks and bonds are doing well. The trick is identifying those periods.

If only we had a yardstick or, better still, a barometer that would show us when to get into commodities and when to stay away. If such a barometer existed, then we could refine Dr. Lintner's theory to a point where commodities weren't just offsetting stocks and bonds, but were themselves a major source of profit.

The barometer that I found was gold.

GOLD—THE NEGATIVE CORRELATION

Gold is a commodity and is traded in several exchanges. (I'm not suggesting that you should necessarily buy gold— only that you should follow its price movements closely.) More importantly, gold is also a currency.

Since antiquity, gold has been a currency of established value. The Egyptians knew of gold, the Romans used it, and it was treasured during the Middle Ages. During the First and Second World Wars many French families survived occupation only because they were able to use gold coins, which they had hoarded, to buy food and protection at a time when their regular currency had no value.

There's no money that speaks louder than gold.

King Faisal

Even today, major countries—including the United States—produce legal tender gold coins. South Africa has the Krugerrand, Australia the Nugget, Canada the Maple Leaf, and the United States the Eagle.

When other currencies fail, gold has always retained its value. That's why in Brazil today (the economics of which we discussed in the last chapter) gold retains its buying power while the cruzero deteriorates.

Because of gold's status as the "currency of last resort," as the only money to retain its buying power, it has a unique position in the world of finance. Gold has become the ultimate negative correlation to the economy.

When there is a threat to our economy, whether it is from inflation or banking collapse or military adventure, where do people turn financially? Do they immediately try to save paper dollars? Do they buy stocks and bonds? Do they go into real estate?

Those in the know do only one thing. They buy gold. Knowledgeable investors convert their assets to gold at the threat of any economic upheaval. This is why each time there is even just the hint of inflation rising, according to "official" sources, gold moves upward. When the U.S. warships entered the Persian Gulf on their "peace keeping" mission, gold rose in price. When Brazil or Mexico or Argentina or some other Third World country threatens to default on its loans, gold goes up. When the stock market falls, gold rises.

Gold is negatively correlated with the economy. In good times, gold does badly. In bad times, gold does very well indeed.

That's why I suggest that gold can be that barometer which we use to gage our investments. We don't necessarily have to invest in gold. We just need to keep track of what it's doing.

On that day that gold moves up in price, that's the day we should begin investing more heavily in commodities. On the day that gold jumps $25 an ounce, that's the day we should consider realigning our investments so that we have less of a commitment to stocks and bonds and more of a commitment in commodities. On that week that gold goes up $25 or more an ounce per day *every day*, that's the week we should consider dumping all our other investments and doing nothing but investing in commodities.

MPT VS. DR. LINTNER

Dr. Lintner's study demonstrates that commodities can be a safe investment as part of an overall portfolio of 40 percent stocks, 40 percent bonds, and 20 percent commodities. The leverage, liquidity, and negative correlation of commodities would offset losses in stocks and bonds, while during good times, gains in stocks and bonds would offset losses in commodities. Dr. Lintner showed how to take some of the volatility, and hence the risk, out of investing.

MPT carries this a step further. In my newsletter I frequently advise my clients to change that ratio. When it appears that inflation, hard times, or some other problem is rearing its head and chomping down on the economy, I have suggested investing as much as 40 or 50 percent in commodities, with the remainder of the portfolio in stocks, bonds, special situations, and real estate.

He who hesitates is lost.

Anonymous

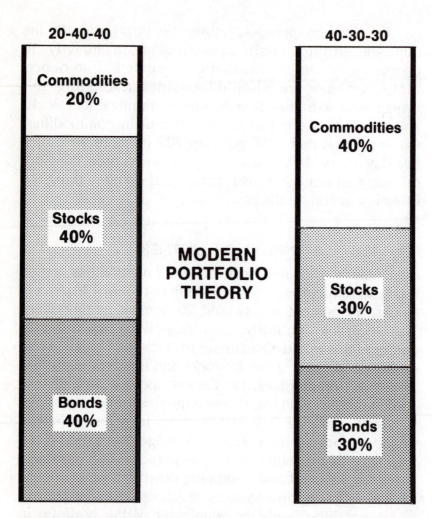

Modern Portfolio Theory juggles the ratios of commodities, stocks, and bonds to increase the profit potential.

I can easily foresee a time when the gold barometer shoots up when I might advise 90 to 100 percent investment in commodities. Because in that situation, the only place where you won't lose money will be the commodities future market.

THE BOTTOM LINE

Are commodities safe?

As part of a balanced portfolio in the manner described by Dr. Lintner, yes, I think they are safe. Their leverage and liquidity make them safe when balanced with other investments such as stocks and bonds. As part of the MPT which I advocate, yes, I think they are safe.

Does that mean that you won't lose money in commodities? No, it doesn't. Even in an inflationary period with gold giving clear signals by price increases, even following Dr. Lintner's theories or MPT, you could lose your shirt. You could go broke if you're in that 85 percent who are at the bottom of the learning curve. You could go broke if you try to invest in commodities on your own and don't know what you are doing. You could lose every penny you put in if you choose the wrong broker, the wrong money manager, or the wrong financial advisor.

But please keep in mind that what I am saying is that if you lose money, it's your fault, not the fault of commodities. Remember, for every dollar lost, there is a dollar won. Commodities is a zero sum game. Somebody is *always* winning. Often that person is winning big.

In the next chapters we'll see how to avoid losing and how to win big in commodities futures.

5

UNDERSTANDING YOUR WEAKNESSES

The weakest person (and, incidentally, also the most foolish) is the one who says he has no weaknesses. In commodities a person who believes he has no weaknesses will also very quickly become the poorest.

There's always the very real possibility that you could be wrong.

B. R.

At the outset, it's important to grasp the fundamental truth that commodities are an emotional investment. The volatility, with prices changing moment to moment requiring numerous quick decisions, makes it so. (This is the reason that when looking for a money manager, always ask to see an *actual* track record, not a *simulated* track record. Simulations show how a system would have operated in the market if it had been used. Usually these come out as shining examples of profit. An actual track record is how a system did perform in the market with real people managing it for real money. It's the only true measurement.)

In the emotionally charged climate of commodities, each of us has our own personal investment weaknesses—you have yours and I have mine—and I don't intend to get into those. However, we all have certain investment weaknesses in common and in this chapter I intend to expose two of them: greed and fear.

WHEN I GOT STARTED

The best way I can think of to illustrate these weaknesses is to describe my own experiences, wild though they might have been, when I got started in commodities. I probably made every mistake and hit every bonanza there was. I think this example should prove illustrative.

Back in 1969 I was a stock broker, having worked for McGraw-Hill (as the youngest managing director they had ever had). I quit McGraw-Hill because overnight I began making triple my former salary.

At the time, I wanted nothing to do with commodities. To me it was the proverbial crapshoot, and anybody who got involved with it was a nut. Besides, I just didn't understand commodities then. Rather than take the time to learn, it was a lot easier to say, "That's just like going to Las Vegas." (Reread the last chapter if you think that statement is correct!)

At the time—this was 1969 and 1970—I began to make big money, well into six figures, and as a result, I had big tax consequences. (If you'll remember the time, it was a bear market, but I was doing hedges and warrants for my accounts and myself and thereby virtually creating a new source of profits. But, that's another story for another book.) At the time it didn't escape my notice that my income resulted in my paying something over two-thirds of my earnings in taxes.

So I talked to the partners of the firm I worked for, and one of them explained that I could use the commodity market to convert ordinary income to long-term capital gains. In short, I would end up paying at a far lower tax rate. (Don't get too steamed up about this strategy—the I.R.S. managed to do away with it several years ago—I'm just explaining it to show how I literally "backed into" commodities.)

The minute the partner said commodities, I yawned and started to lose interest. But the tax problem wasn't going to go away, and the more the partner explained, the more I got interested.

Napoleon Hill said, "Work always for 'onemanship.'" He meant always have only one goal and wait until it's finished before you start the next.

B. R.

The basic strategy was to buy gold in the physical market and sell it short in the futures market. By borrowing on the physical purchase from a bank and by closing out the short position on December 31 and opening it again in January 1, you were able to deduct all the carrying charges on the physical gold, while offsetting them in the futures market. The net result was that you got a huge deduction for carrying charges which, if you played the strategy well, was enough to offset your entire income!

I was hooked onto commodities. I didn't get into the business to make a profit. I did it to legally reduce my taxes.

Shortly thereafter I ran into a gentleman who was a Cuban national. He had come over to this country with basically no money, but he still had his Cuban contacts and he came from an extremely wealthy family with sugar processing interests. This man was investing in sugar futures.

The only thing I knew about sugar was that you put it into your coffee. Anyhow, relying on his knowledge of sugar, I bought four contracts of my own which back in 1971 cost $2,000.

The importance of this investment was that it was not a tax move. It was my first for-profit venture into commodities. (Actually, I was making well into six figures, I had bought a big house and car and was living fairly well. As a result, even though I was making plenty of money, I was still broke! It's a common phenomenon amongst the newly rich.)

I actually used my MasterCard to borrow the $2,000 I put up for the sugar contracts! I bought sugar at two cents. Soon after, it went up to four cents.

During the time it went from two to four cents, I bought additional contracts. (This is called pyramiding, and I'll show you why you *shouldn't* do it in a later chapter.)

You have to understand that I wasn't acting as a commodity broker at the time. I was investing my money with another broker who made the commissions. I was doing this on my own.

If I had real savvy of the market, I could probably have made half a million dollars during this run-up. As it was, because of the *leverage* available in commodities, I made $45,000 in one year on a $2,000 investment.

I had never seen money come in like that before. All I knew was that this kid was getting into commodities. I got licensed as a commodities broker.

A man's reach should always exceed his grasp.

Of course, I had never "been to the well." In commodities lingo that means that I hadn't seen my account nor my clients' accounts lose all their equities in bad trades. I had only seen the sunny side of commodities, and I had no idea things could go wrong. I thought commodities was the easiest way to make money that I had ever run into, and I couldn't understand why I'd never found it before.

(Incidentally, my MBA is from Columbia University and Columbia's School of Business was one of the first to have an actual commodities department. You can get an education in commodities at Columbia, and I had been there earning an MBA and had been aware of these programs and still hadn't wanted to trade commodities!)

After making $45,000 on a $2,000 investment, however, I was a "done dog." With the advice of a Ph.D. in agro-economics, I went into grains. He laid out this fundamental case that wheat, soybeans, and corn were going to go up because of the fundamental supply and demand relationship.

I popped my whole $45,000 into the grains. As it turned out, the Russians had secretly bought up all our grain reserves. (It wasn't a secret from our government—they're the ones who hushed it up. It was a secret from the general public.)

Roughly eighteen months later I had transformed that original $2,000 borrowed on a credit card into $1.2 million. At that point, I quit the market for reasons I'll explain shortly.

GREED—THE GREAT MOTIVATOR

It's important to be perfectly clear about why I got into the commodities market, why I opened contracts, why I took the risks involved. The answer, plain and simple, was greed.

I wanted to make money, lots of money. I wanted to make it quickly and easily, and commodities was the avenue I found for making it.

Greed is usually considered an undesirable quality to have. The truth, however, if we're man (or woman) enough to admit it, is that we all have greed. If the opportunity to make big bucks with a minimum amount of risk and effort presents itself, we will take it. I have yet to meet a person who will give up the opportunity to make a quick profit.

Greed, the desire for profit, is what motivates people to get into the commodities market. Perhaps we see an opportunity in grains. We realize that for a few thousand dollars, we stand to make $20,000 or more on a single contract. So we begin to trade.

That is exactly what happened in my case. The typical story of someone who begins trading commodities is that they stumble onto it. Once they see the money to be made, they are hooked for life.

There's only one rule for success, only one way to express it—persist.

B. R.

THE OTHER SIDE OF THE MARKET

Thus far we have been discussing the up side of the market, the profit potential that tickles our greed and gets us started trading commodities. There is, however, a down side, as I noted earlier. I ran into this as well, albeit in a most strange manner.

On the way to making $1.2 million in 18 months, I took a very strange turn. I was establishing a heavy position in grain. I called up the trading department in the firm where I was working and gave them a complex order based on a technical signal. Essentially the order said this: "I want to buy wheat or corn or soybeans or soybean meal or soybean oil or a half dozen other grains. I want to buy *one* of these, and here's how I want you to determine which one it is that I buy. I am giving you a certain price. If they start moving up in price, the first one that hits that price, buy it. Then cancel all the rest." (This is technically called a "stop-buy" order.)

Be sure you understand what I was ordering. I wanted to end up with a contract in only *one* commodity. I was leaving the choice of which commodity to end up in to the broker. He was to make the decision based on which of the group of commodities I'd selected made the biggest move upward first.

Confident that I had placed my order, I left town to attend a business meeting in another city. Of course, the broker in the trading department had misunderstood my order!

The following Monday I was still out of town, and I called in to see if my order had been placed. I about had a heart attack when I heard what had happened. Yes, the prices had gone up. However, instead of placing a contract for *one* commodity, the broker had put me into all of them! I had open contracts in virtually every grain across the board. My exposure, in terms of loss, was potentially hundreds of thousands of dollars.

FEAR—THE OTHER SIDE OF THE COIN

If greed had motivated me to get into the market, fear was pushing me to get out. Here I was looking at a potential loss of hundreds of thousands of dollars, of my entire equity. For the first time, I was looking at going to the well . . . and I saw that the well could come up dry.

My mind went blank, and all that greed that had been pushing me to invest was instantly gone. "Out," I told myself. "You've got to get out before you're killed." I tasted fear.

I counted to ten and then counted again to try to get my pulse steady. Then, with my fingers shaking, I called up the senior partner of the firm. As soon as he got on the phone, I blurted out what happened and then said, "Our broker made a horrible mistake. He did not fill the order the way I wanted. I want out. I'm not accepting these trades, because it could kill me. I just want out." I must confess that looking back on it, my request must have sounded more like a plaintive demand. However, I was consumed with fear.

At this point the senior partner laughed and said, "That's perfectly fine. However, would you mind if I take them on . . . they are *all currently up the limit!*"

I did a quick calculation. All the contracts up the limit made me a fast $600,000!

I tried searching my mind for that fear that just a very few moments earlier had been devouring my being. It had suddenly become a very insignificant, very small thing. In fact, I couldn't even find it! Very quietly I said back into the telephone, "No, I believe I'll keep them."

A bull sometimes makes money. A bear sometimes makes money. But a pig never does.

Roy Longstreet

I hung up and thought about it. With a sappy, satisfied smile, I turned to a friend nearby and told him that I was the boy wonder of commodities. It was my great ability in the markets and my tremendous knowledge that had made me a fortune overnight. (Remember, this was back in the early 1970s when a hundred thousand was more like a million.)

Wasn't I smart, I told myself. And the more I told myself, the more I believed it. And the more I believed, the more I began to think that if I could make $600,000 over the weekend, why couldn't I make another $600,000 during the next week? Greed, which had been obliterated by fear, came roaring back.

I called the trading broker back and told him, "Leave the contracts on."

True to form, as soon as I said this, fear again crept up. Leaving the contracts on left me still exposed. If the price turned, I could still lose everything I had made and more. So I added, "On the first sign of weakness in the market, sell it all out . . . I'll take my profit."

Mind you, I've just made $600,000 on an error. All I have to do is to sell it all out immediately and I can pocket the cash. But greed tells me that I'm so smart, I can stay in the market and make another $600,000 by tomorrow. Fear tells me to protect myself, so I tell the broker to sell it out if the price starts to fall.

Now I've taken care of both fear and greed and I'm one self-satisfied slaphappy fellow.

THE DARK DAYS

I hung up and decided to spend the afternoon playing bridge. (In those days I was an avid bridge player, and not too bad at the game if I say so myself.)

I hung up at approximately 11:00 in the morning. The grain markets closed at 12:15. The bridge game wouldn't start until 12:00, so I went across the street and bought myself a new Cadillac. I just wrote out a check for the most expensive car in the dealership, intending to pay for it with equity from my commodities account. (Remember, you can withdraw your profits at any time.) This was really a thrill for me because it was the very first time I had ever paid for a car with cash.

I shall return.

General Douglas MacArthur

Off I go to play bridge. We had just started on the first rubber when I get a telephone call from my secretary. I go to the phone thinking she is about to tell me how much richer I am. Instead, she informs me that at ten minutes past 12:00, five minutes before the markets close, the markets all reversed and *went down the limit!*

I sat down rather abruptly. Down the limit meant I could have lost as much as I had made. However, I tried to calm the butterflies in my stomach. I had told the broker to "take me out at the first sign of weakness." Hopefully he had. I was praying, "Dear Lord, let me not be in the market."

I left the bridge tournament and went to my office where I called the broker. This is what he told me had basically happened. The markets had turned so suddenly that there were no traders on the other side. He had tried to get me out, but he couldn't do it before the closing bell. I was still in . . . and down the limit!

My heart sank. In just a few hours I had gone from congratulating myself on my ingenuity to kicking myself for my stupidity.

THE MORAL

I was finally able to get out. The next few days the markets were down the limit. But by borrowing a huge sum of money, I was able to do an offsetting trade in the cash markets (the markets closest to the spot or current month which have no trading limits) and trade out. (By the way, this is a strategy that you may want to keep in reserve if you ever get trapped in a limit move.)

Never continue only *because you have begun.*

B. R.

When it was all over my equity position was $480,000. Not bad you might say? Consider, had I taken $2,000 up to $480,000 in eighteen months? Or had I taken $1.2 million down to $480,000 in a few days?

My first wife told me I had taken $1.2 million down to $480,000 and shortly thereafter divorced me to make sure I didn't lose any more of her money. My own personal feeling is the other way round. I think I took that $2,000 up to nearly half a million.

Regardless of whether you think I was a hero or a bum because of this trading, you should see what this story teaches. It shows that the main motivating emotional forces in commodities are fear and greed. Greed got me in, fear got me out. It happened to me that way . . . and when you get into commodities (if you're not already trading, it will, I guarantee it will, happen to you.)

If you think about it, fear and greed motivate those who don't even get into commodities. The reason I stayed out of commodities initially was that I didn't really understand them. I couldn't really explain what trading was. Every time I invested in something, my wife would ask me, "Well, why did you do it?" I'd give her the supply and the demand fundamentals and she'd understand. But, what if I went home and said, "Dear, I invested in soybean oil."

She would surely ask, "What's soybean oil?" I would have to say, I haven't got the slightest idea!" And that made me afraid. So, initially I stayed out of the market. It was only when, virtually by accident, I made money in the market, that greed took over and nudged me in.

THE IMPORTANCE OF DISCIPLINE

A successful trader learns to have a system that in effect controls greed and fear. True discipline, if I'd had it, would have been for me to have sold out the minute that I found out that there had been a mistake made, because true discipline would have demanded that I stick to my predetermined trading program. (Remember, that program said I should be in *one* commodity, not all of them. If I had been in one and it was down the limit, I wouldn't have sustained anywhere near as great a loss.)

> *You must have a program. You must know your program. You must follow your program.*
>
> Roy W. Longstreet

The moment something happens that is different than the trading program, than the system, dictates, I should have liquidated. Had I done so, I would have been up $600,000—a gift from God.

In the next chapters we are going to look at the elements of trading systems. However, before doing that, let me make a point that I'll return to again and again. Very few people have the necessary discipline to stick to a trading program even once they get one. Far too often, greed or fear motivates us to forget our discipline.

HOW TO MAINTAIN PERFECT DISCIPLINE

To conclude my story, after I got out of the grain trades, I quit the commodity business for a time. I went to Hawaii, rented a room at a fine hotel, sat on the beach with a drink, and thought.

My conclusion was that I, personally, was not suited to trade my own account. I, personally, was too susceptible to the swings of fear and greed. In other words, I could not trust myself not to abandon my trading program when things either went unexpectedly well . . . or unexpectedly badly.

Did that mean that I should get out of commodities? Hardly. I had made over a million dollars (although I kept less than half of it) in less than 18 months of trading. Obviously, commodities was the avenue that was going to lead to my ultimate fortune. I just had to find a different vehicle to get me there.

The vehicle I selected was a manager who handled the trades for me.

It's important to understand that what I'm talking about here is significantly different than what I've discussed up to this point. Prior to this, I had been calling up the broker and telling him, "Trade me into this." Or, "Trade me out of that."

My trades, of course, had been predicted on both fundamental as well as technical information. Nevertheless, I was the one who essentially executed them. I was the one who picked up the phone and said what to buy or sell and when.

What I decided to do was to give up that responsibility. I would give it to someone else, someone I would hand pick.

That didn't meant that I was going to let that person have a field day with my money. Quite the contrary. I would work out a plan, a system. I would give that person very strict parameters. He would be able to trade this or that on his own. However, he had to follow the system that I dictated. Since it wasn't his money he was playing with, but rather was mine, he shouldn't have to contend with the greed and fear that threw me off.

It was a great plan, and back in the early 1970s, it set a precedent. I helped develop a system, later computerized, which a major brokerage house is still using to this day that allows them to trade commodities successfully.

Of course, I don't expect that you, the reader, will be much interested in developing a computerized trading system. In fact, you shouldn't. It would be like reinventing the wheel. Today, there are brokerage houses across the country that operate super-sophisticated systems that profitably trade their customers in and out of commodities.

What you need to do is to find the right person and give him or her the right parameters with regards to trading your account. Once you do that, you will have established a way of getting the discipline necessary to successfully trade commodities.

GREED AND FEAR

It's important to remember that greed and fear are always going to be with you when you trade commodities. The way to get around their influence is to have someone else handle the trades for you. In later chapters, we will see how to find the correct person to trade your account. But first, in the next chapter we will look at the ten basic strategies you need to know in order to formulate the instruction you will give to your ultimate commodities trader.

6

TEN STRATEGIES
FOR PROFITING
IN COMMODITIES

*There ain't no easy money lying around . . . and if there
is, ain't nobody trying to shove it into your pocket.*

Jesse Livermore

Jesse Livermore became famous in the financial world for
making $9 million shorting stocks going into the Great
Depression. Then he took his $9 million and ran it up
to $20 million in the commodities market. Mind you, this
was in 1929 and 1930 when most financial whiz kids were
jumping out of the windows of tall buildings.

Jesse became a sort of legend, a person who those
in the industry looked up to. During the dark days of the
Great Depression, Jesse was like a ray of hope.

In 1931 Jesse Livermore shot himself in the men's
room of the Roosevelt Hotel in New York City. The reason?
He had taken his $20 million down to $2 million in later
trades in commodities.

Keep in mind that during the Great Depression, even $2 million wasn't so bad. However, it was the thought of losing that $18 million that had been in his pocket that did Jesse in.

As it turned out, Jesse Livermore did most of those things that you shouldn't do in commodities. He pyramided his money. He got "married to his positions." He pulled out without letting his winners ride. There are some who say that the money he made at first was just a fluke . . . that Jesse, in reality, never really had a chance in the commodities market.

Maybe they're right. Most of the people I've seen who are the big losers were the ones who started out as the big winners. They, so to speak, fell into it. But once in, they didn't know how to keep their winnings coming.

A compulsive trader is too much in love with the market.

B. R.

In this chapter we're going to look at ten separate strategies. Each one is a lesson in itself. Each one tells a story. Each one is a "must." If you absorb all ten and follow them to the letter, there's no way you can lose in commodities—I guarantee it!

STRATEGY I—GO ONLY FOR THE TWO OR THREE TRADES *A YEAR* THAT CAN MAKE YOU MONEY

I have a friend who told me that his commodity broker wants him to put up enough cash so that he can make a minimum of five trades each time he goes into the market.

The broker tells him that you have to keep hitting at a position until you get a winner.

This friend ended up making 27 trades his first three months in commodities. The result, he was down $2,500, which I consider very lucky. He could have been down one heck of a lot more making that many trades.

The first rule of commodity trading is that every single year, at least on one or two commodities make a major price advance or a major price decline based on supply and demand factors alone. This has nothing to do with inflation or deflation. It happens whether the commodities market is hot or cold. (Of course, if it's hot, then there are many more than one or two opportunities.)

Any broker worth his salt should be able to find those one or two trades. If your broker can't identify those big price swings based on fundamentals, then he shouldn't be anywhere near the business.

If you're starting out in commodities, or even if you've been in them a while, you should put your $2,000 or $3,000 or whatever in the account and then patiently wait. Read the *Wall Street Journal* and *Investor's Daily* every day. Read about the weather in the Midwest, and the grain forecasts, and the supply and demand factors in copper. Read about the cattle feeding and frosts in the Florida orange juice belt. Don't trade . . . read!

Never aim lower than the stars.

Eventually you'll know what's going on in commodities and, if you're relying on a broker and he's any good, one day he'll call and say that there's an opportunity in copper . . . or in silver . . . or in orange juice . . . or whatever.

It might be three months or six months before he calls. But when he does, from all your reading, you'll know that he's right. And you'll make your trade.

If you've done your homework and if you've waited patiently and if this is in fact the big move for the year in a commodity, you'll make your $10,000 or $20,000 *per contract* and you'll be feeling mighty smug.

By the way, your total commission paid should be no more than a couple hundred dollars!

STRATEGY 2—USE A COMPUTER SYSTEM

The worst thing any investor can do is to try and reinvent the wheel. You could spend years trying to develop a technical system based on market signals and if, and that's a big IF, you were successful, you'd only end up duplicating some probably superior system that's already out there. Of course, it's imperative that you fully understand what a computerized commodities investing system does.

Most computerized systems are based on technical signals. Technical signals are indications of what the market may do based solely on past price movements. While at first this may sound simple, it's actually quite complex.

Computerized systems not only watch the raw price performance of commodities; they also watch such things as moving averages. (Moving averages are typically based on 3, 5, 10, or 30 days. You add up the closing prices for each of the days in the period and then divide by the period. For example, on a 3-day moving average, you would add up the prices of the last three days and then divide by three. You would do this *every day*. We'll have a much more detailed explanation of this in a later chapter.)

In addition to keeping track of moving averages, the computers also watch patterns in price performance. We'll have a lot more to say about this in the chapter on charting. However, for now, let's just say that the computer compares current patterns in prices with historical patterns in prices.

A computer is like an "idiot savant"—it only knows a little bit. But it knows that better than anybody else.

B. R.

When the computer recognizes a pattern that indicates that the price is likely to go higher or lower in the immediate future, it sends a buy or sell signal to the broker. Brokers who follow these computer models then immediately buy or sell. (Sophisticated computer systems today actually generate the buy/sell orders themselves!)

Back in the early 1970s, with the assistance of a computer specialist, I created one of the first computer systems approved for commodity trading called TLA. This system used a complex formula for tracking moving averages and other pricing patterns. Today it is used by a major commodities firm to handle millions of dollars of transactions.

The important point to understand here, however, is that sharp commodity brokers and successful houses use sophisticated computer systems, and if you don't take advantage of them, you're missing the boat.

This is not to say that by arduous study and careful analysis, you can't do what the computers do. You can. But as I said at the outset, why reinvent the wheel? The computer systems are already in place. Take advantage of them.

Having thus touted the wonders of computers, let me end by noting the negative side. Today, so much trading is done by computer systems that the systems themselves influence the market. Often the various systems will all recognize a particular market fluctuation as a trend. When that happens, many of the systems simultaneously will send buy or sell signals out and an enormous amount of trading suddenly takes place. That's why for no apparent reason in any given day you may see the price of pork bellies jump up or the price of silver plummet. The computers are trying to get their masters in at the beginning of a trend.

What you should know is that *the computers are wrong 60 percent of the time*. That's correct, the best systems only work 40 percent of the time. Having said that, I'm sure many readers are wondering why I resort to computers that are so fallible? The answer is part of the next strategy.

STRATEGY 3—LET YOUR WINNERS RIDE

This is probably the first rule that most new traders learn about commodities. When you have a winner, let the profits ride. When you have a loser, dump it quickly.

It's simply said, and it would appear to be a simple rule to follow, but it's not. Let me give an example of why not.

Those who let their profits ride, last.

P. O.

Let's say you're trading currencies, for instance, the Japanese yen. You've gone long on the yen and the dollar is down, meaning the yen is up. Yesterday your account showed a $5,000 profit.

Today, the U.S. government intervenes. The dollar rises and the yen falls. Your account is down to a $3,000 profit. Your broker calls and tells you that the yen might fall even further. Then he says the seven most unholy words in commodity trading, "You can't go broke taking a profit."

Remember, greed brought you into the market and got you trading to begin with. You've made a profit; now you fear that you'll lose that profit. Those seven words your broker utters strike deep at your fear.

But, you ask, what if the market turns and the yen skyrockets? Won't I lose out on bigger profits?

To this your broker smugly replies, "You can always get back in."

So you close out your position and take your $3,000 profit. And at the end of trading that day the yen skyrockets . . . and you can't get back in! By tomorrow your profits would have been $6,000, the next day $9,000, and so on. But you've missed the train on this trip. You're out.

Of course, you say, I made $3,000 profit. Why should I worry?

You should worry because, as we saw in the last example, the very best computerized systems, which make trades far better than you alone can, are wrong 60 percent of the time. The only way you can make up for the 60 percent loss is to let those 40 percent winners ride. You may lose $1,000 or $2,000 each time on those 60 percent losers. Consequently, you better make $20,000 or more on those 40 percent winners!

The truth of this really came home to me a few years back when an account I had decided to really test the system. He reasoned that if the computers were wrong 60 percent of the time, let's do the *opposite* of what the computer says. When the computer says buy, we sell. When it says sell, we buy. As a result we'll be right 60 percent of the time instead of 40. We'll have to make money!

When everyone is bearish, it means that there's no one left to sell. When everyone is bullish, it means that there's no one left to buy.

The contrarian view

Sound like a good idea? Be sure you understand what's involved before you answer. The computer systems are constantly giving buy/sell signals. Now, instead of following those signals—because you know from past experience that they are wrong 60 percent of the time— you trade exactly opposite. That should make you a loser only 40 percent of the time. Winning more than half should be enough to let you ride to glory on your profits.

The person who did this used the old Commodity Research Bureau system, a competent computer model. The guy comes in and tells me that he has figured out a way to wealth. So we start doing it. After all, I was fascinated. What he said was logical. What if he was right? We could all make a fortune overnight.

The only thing was, he had to be quick in his trades. He had to dump the losers on the first sign of weakness. After all, he was betting against what the computers suggested.

In the initial days of using his system, it was fun. We made a heck of a lot of trades, and he was making a decent little return on his money, something like 30 or 40 percent annualized.

At the end of a year, however, he had made nothing. His account, in fact, was down from all the commission costs of all those trades. The computer system for that year, however, was up over 100 percent in profits.

Why? The computer was wrong 60 percent of the time. Yet, it made a 100 percent profit. The account, by going opposite to the computer, had to be right 60 percent of the time, but lost money. How could that be?

Consider how it works. The computer is only telling you what the price trend is. The computer says "buy" and we all jump in and buy. But six times out of ten the computer is wrong and the price moves against us, so we all jump out.

But those four out of ten times that the computer is right, it has pegged a *trend*. With a trend, once you're out, you can't get back in—the price movement is too far, too strong, too quick.

To put it another way, 40 percent of the time the computer picks the BIG winners. If you let those big winners ride, they more than compensate for the 60 percent of the time the computer is wrong.

On the other hand, if you go into those trades where the computer is wrong 60 percent of the time, they are small trades. There is no trend. There are no profits to let ride.

Thus, when we say that the computer is wrong 60 percent of the time, it means that the trend signals fail to materialize. Forty percent of the time, however, that trend does materialize and if you are in there and *if you let that winner ride*, you are on the road to riches.

The whole message of this strategy is to let your winners ride. You may go up, and then you may go all the way back down to zero. You may lament the money that you "lost" on the ride. But you're not trying to make money on the short rides. You're trying to identify the big roller coaster, the trend that will make you bundles. You'll never get rich off hiccups in the market. What you need is a full blown explosion.

STRATEGY 4—DIVERSIFY WITHIN COMMODITIES

There's a classic story told of an investor who made several hundred thousand dollars in a few weeks back in 1980. At that time we saw the biggest surge in silver prices in history. Silver went from around $6 an ounce to $50 in an incredibly short time. (Of course, from there it went back to $6, which provides another truism—a commodity always returns to its point [previous price]. But that's a story for another book.)

This investor who made the couple of hundred thousand in silver figured he had finally found the road paved with golden bricks. He quit his job and took up residence at his broker's office. His full-time career, now, would be investing in commodities. Not just any commodities, but silver, a market he felt he knew very well.

You may just as easily be right for the wrong reasons, as wrong for the right reasons.

B. R.

The last time I saw him, he was applying for welfare. Silver went eight years without another dramatic move. Oh sure, it had its ups and downs, and he made money here and there. But the big moves that made him his hundreds of thousands just didn't happen again.

This is not to say that silver won't return to $50 an ounce. I absolutely believe it will. A commodity always returns to its point (previous price). However, it may not do it until the middle of the next century for all I know.

The point here is that this individual specialized in just one commodity, and that was his downfall. As noted in strategy one, there are one or two major moves every year based strictly on supply and demand. But those moves are almost never repeated in the same commodity. In the summer it may be soybeans; in the winter it may be copper. The next summer it might be pork bellies and so forth.

If you specialize in just one commodity or just one area of commodities such as grains or metals, you may go broke waiting for lightning to strike your field. On the other hand, it may be striking like crazy in your neighbor's yard.

When you enter commodities, you have to determine that you are in all commodities. You will trade wherever the big move is. Put simply, you need to be willing to diversify your trades.

If you're a big investor with $50,000 to $100,000, you can diversify all over the board. If you're a small investor with under $5,000, then you'll just have to be patient. You'll have to follow all the commodities and pick the winners (and hope that you've made the right choice).

Many computer systems handle diversification for you. They automatically put you into the commodity which offers the best chance of being caught in a major move.

Diversifying by investing in several computer systems works even better. Here you have your capital spread among several models, and if any of them hit, you're a big winner.

Of course, you need to set up limits. I'll discuss limits in a later chapter, but for now I just want to talk about one kind of limit that is absolutely necessary in diversification through computer systems.

Limiting Diversification by Computer System

Remember, the computer is not a thinking being. It's just a machine which follows the program that's been placed in it to the letter. In almost all cases, the program is designed to identify trends. The very success of that program, however, can be your undoing.

Consider currencies as an example. You can trade in Japanese yen, German deutsche marks, British pounds, Swiss francs, French francs and so forth. The point is that there are a lot of different individual currencies under the general heading of currency.

What you need to know is that very frequently all the currencies will react together. The reason, quite simply, is that they are used to short the U.S. dollar. How do you short (sell) dollars when you don't own dollars? Simple, you buy the currency of some other nation. What that means is that when dollars go down in value, the value of other currencies goes up.

The computer, however, doesn't necessarily know this. The computer program is designed to identify trends. So on Monday the dollar begins to fall and the Japanese yen is up. Suddenly the computer signals that you should buy yen, so you go long in yen.

Always strive to diversify. But always be sure you haven't diversified all into the same area.

B. R.

By mid-morning, the German mark is up and the computer sends another signal, so you go long in marks.

By noon, there's a general run on the dollar and the computer signals to go long francs, pounds, and every other currency. Do you do it?

Not if you have a half a brain in your head.

You might get a dozen different buy signals from a dozen different commodities. But in reality, they are all one signal. They are all signaling one thing only, that the dollar is falling. If you heed all those signals and buy all the commodities, you haven't limited your exposure and increased your chances of profit through diversification. Instead you've increased your exposure and limited your chances of profit through concentration. All of your contracts will depend on one thing—the dollar. That's not diversification in my book.

If the dollar reverses and moves upward, all those contracts will also reverse and you'll lose big bucks. You have to understand that many commodities are *linked*. The currencies are linked and often move in tandem. The same holds true for the grains, the precious metals, livestock, financial instruments, and other areas.

What I do is tell my broker, who can then plug it into the computer system, that if there's a signal to buy or sell in one commodity, such as yen, go ahead and do a trade. If there's another signal in a *linked* commodity, do another trade. But after that, *ignore any further signals from linked commodities*. In our example, I might be in yen and deutsche marks. But that's all. If there is a trend and the computer was correct, I'll make plenty. But, if the computer was wrong and it's not the start of a trend, only a market hiccup, I've limited my exposure.

Yes, you want to diversify. But you don't want to diversify all over Hell's half acre. You want to be sure you're ready to trade in any commodity that signals it's making a major move. You don't want to trade in all the linked commodities in that field.

STRATEGY 5—TRADE SMALL IF YOU'RE A SMALL INVESTOR

Quite frankly you need a minimum of $50,000 to trade effectively by computer. Most investors, however, don't have $50,000. Rather, they have closer to $5,000 or less. (It's a fact that in this country less than 8 percent of the population can write a check for $10,000 without first calling the bank and arranging for a loan.)

Never get into trades that are over your head.

B. R.

If you're a small investor starting out, there are two strategies that I advocate you consider—pooling and waiting for special situations. We'll consider them separately.

Pooling

A "pool" is a legal designation. It involves pooling a bunch of money from different investors. Instead of having one investor with $50,000, you pool ten investors with $5,000. The risk is the same and the return is proportionately the same. (If the single big investor makes 50 percent on his money, or loses 50 percent, the small investor does the same percentage.)

To run a pool, the operator must be registered as a pool broker with the Commodity Futures Authority and must meet a series of fairly strict requirements. In the previous examples I've given of people getting into commodities, their names were on the account in the brokerage house. In the case of a pool, the pool's name is on the account. The money is insured, and there is virtually no possibility of fraud or of getting the pooled money confused with other money. In other words, in a pool you are normally just as safe as you would be in an individual account.

When you go into a pool you're joining up with 10 or 30 or maybe 200 or 300 other people. The money is no longer in your name, but you get all the benefits.

And the benefits can be significant. Most importantly, a pool has enough clout to afford a good money manager with a good computer system. For a small investment, you're playing right up there with the big boys.

There are, however, some problems with pools. Basically, brokers don't like them. Why don't brokers like pools? It's simple. Consider, if you have 20 investors and they each make a trade, how many commissions do you get? Twenty, right? On the other hand, if 20 people pool their money, how many commissions are there to make? That's right, only one. A pool is not a very advantageous way to handle investors from a broker's perspective.

On the other hand, firms love pools. Brokerage houses want you to go into pools that they've organized so that they get control of the money and have captive commissions. They promote pools as commodity's version of a mutual fund or a limited partnership. Unfortunately, that's not always the case. These could end up being nothing more than churning pools where the profits are all eaten up by the commissions.

What you want, therefore, is what's hardest to find. You want a pool that's run in such a way that the parameters are to your liking—few trades, maximized computerized assistance. How do you find such pools?

No question, it takes a lot of searching. In later chapters we'll go into methods of finding brokers and money managers who can direct you to good pools.

Special Situations

The other method of investing in commodities if you don't have more than a few thousand dollars is to open your own account and place your own trades. Of course, you can't possibly diversify. So, instead you have to study the market very carefully and hope that you can identify those one or two major moves a year on your own.

Essentially what you are looking for is a "special situation." By that I mean a trade that's special, one that offers great opportunity. For example, back in 1986 the Chairman of the Federal Reserve board said, "The dollar is too high. We're going to let it drop in value."

Always keep most of your capital in reserve. That way you'll always be ready to take advantage when opportunity calls.

B. R.

Now, there aren't many times in history that the person running the central bank of the most powerful country in the world announces his intentions regarding his currency. If you had your ears open, you would have realized this was a "special situation." Forget supply and demand and technical signals. This is information leading to an almost certain winner. So, if you had your ears open, you went long in yen or deutsche marks or just about any other currency. And for three years you were sitting on the hundreds and hundreds of thousands of dollars you had made.

Special situations don't come up all the time. They don't even come up very often. If you have limited funds, what you have to do is offset that limitation with research, readiness and most important of all, patience.

STRATEGY 6—DON'T PYRAMID

Pyramids fail. Not some pyramids or a few pyramids, but for the average investor, all pyramids fail, period.

What's a pyramid? Let's say you go long in copper with one contract. Copper goes up a few cents a pound and you have a $1,500 profit. Now you have a choice. You can take your money out. Or you can use it to open a new contract in copper.

If you pyramid, you take your money out and use it to open a new contract at the higher price level. If the price goes up, you do it again opening a third contract at a yet higher level.

Each time copper goes up, you use the profits on previous contracts to open new ones. The progression of your investments look like an inverted pyramid.

PYRAMIDING

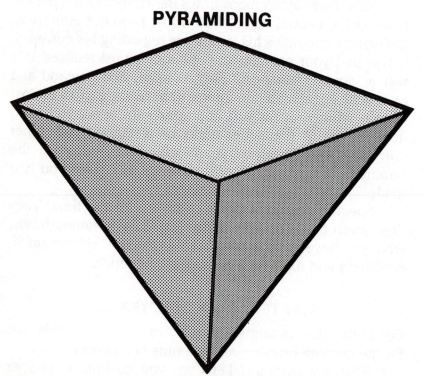

Pyramiding—note that the pyramid is always out of balance, constantly threatening your investment.

What's going to happen? In your mind you're projecting that as long as copper goes up, you'll have more and more contracts on and be making more and more money. Greed (remember the great motivator?) has taken firm hold of your senses.

The problem, of course, is one of timing. You can never know when copper is going to peak out and turn down. In your mind you are always projecting a higher price. But one day copper turns down.

Now you've got losses. Just as you took $1,500 out, you've now got to put $1,500 back in. Only now, you don't have the $1,500! Rather, you've spent it all on the other contracts. You're spread out thin as paper in contracts at ever higher price levels.

All that has to happen is for the price at the top to drop just a fraction, and your whole pyramid comes tumbling down. So now you've lost all the money you would have made, *even though you were right on copper*. If you had simply kept your one original contract, you would have done quite well.

Reverse Pyramids

Reverse pyramids, on the other hand, work quite well. In a reverse pyramid you believe that a commodity is going to make a move. You believe a drought is going to force grain prices up—or that U.S. economic pressures are going to force the dollar down. So you decide to get into the market. You buy soybeans or deutsche marks.

Only instead of opening just one contract, you put as much money into the market as you can. You open two or three or five contracts.

There are old pilots and there are bold pilots, but there are no old, bold pilots.

Air Force motto

On day one we open the contracts. On day two the market moves the way we hoped and we doubled our money. We now trade out one of the contracts. If we had five, we now have four. We've taken some of our profits and reduced our exposure.

On day three the market goes up and we double our money again. We close out another contract, taking our profits.

We keep going in this manner, pulling our money out so that in the worst case scenario, we leave with a profit. By day ten, we may have only one open contract. If the market now turns against us, we may lose a few bucks on that contract, but we will have made a bundle on the other four.

Our scenario looks like a reverse pyramid, which is to say, like a real pyramid. Instead of adding money to the market, we've taken it out. Reverse pyramids do work for the average investor and are a means of controlling exposure and increasing profits.

Pyramiding for the "Not So Average" Investor

Thus far I've been decrying the pyramid while extolling the virtues of the reverse pyramid. As I said, this is virtually always true for the average investor. But for the above average investor, it's a different story. Let me give two cases in point:

In the first case we have a dentist. Here's a fellow who buys gold and silver as part of his business. Because he uses the metal to fill people's teeth, he's aware of the market in a kind of peripheral way.

It is 1979 and the dentist realizes that the silver market is going wild. There are opportunities to profit that may never repeat in history. Silver is on its way up from $6 to an incredible $50 an ounce.

He buys, and as the price goes up, he begins pyramiding his money in the fashion I've described above. As long as silver continues going up, he's making thousands, actually hundreds of thousands.

On the other hand, we have Omar Sharif. Omar Sharif, besides being a famous actor, is also a world class bridge player, a statistician, and an extremely intelligent man. On the other hand, his gambling is legendary and while most people think he's very wealthy, frequently he's quite the opposite.

Sharif is playing in bridge tournaments, and he's also keeping his ear to the wire listening to what's happening in the world of silver. He's making lots of money in the movies, and he decides to enter the silver market, just like my dentist, only with one big difference. Sharif leaves all investing to professionals. He finds a money manager. This is a person who directs the investment of Sharif's money. The money manager doesn't make the investments himself. Rather, he goes out into the market place and finds the very best specialists. Sharif's money manager picks an expert in commodities futures.

Sharif's money manager gives this commodities expert roughly $100,000. Now Sharif has just entered the commodities futures market.

The silver boom continued through 1980 when the rules on margins were changed and the Hunt brothers, who it turns out were later convicted of market manipulation, weren't able to continue buying silver. At that point the price collapsed.

What were the results of the biggest market boom in silver in history for my dentist friend and for Omar Sharif? The dentist came out without a penny! At one time, he had hundreds of thousands of dollars in profit. But because he pyramided, he gave it all back.

Wisdom is the ability to know yourself.

B. R.

What about Sharif? His expert commodities broker, under the watchful eye of his money manager, parlayed his original $100,000 into roughly $4 million. He got out before the market peaked and kept his profits (with which he bought a small casino so he would always have a place to gamble and could always win because he'd be the house).

Let's look at it more closely. Did Sharif's manager pyramid his money? Yes, but very modestly. When his original contracts were up sharply, a small portion of the profits were used to open new contracts. Unlike the dentist, however, his money manager didn't aggressively pyramid all the profits hoping for an even bigger grand slam.

In addition, Sharif didn't pay much attention to the minute-by-minute movements of the market. He generally kept abreast of what was happening and called in occasionally to see how his equity was doing, but kept his distance. He concentrated on playing bridge and making movies.

On the other hand, the dentist virtually gave up his dental practice. Never mind that this was a long-range play in a very unique and special situation. The dentist was on his phone first thing in the morning, before he bathed, talking to his broker to find out how the European markets were doing. Then he made his first daily market decisions.

After a shower, shave, and breakfast, he'd be back on the phone to find out how the New York markets were behaving, and he'd be making more decisions and trades.

He drove to work, saw a few patients, and called again to see what the markets looked like and made more decisions. All during the day he'd be taking breaks and buying and selling on the phone with his broker. At one point he was up over $600,000 in profits! But he stayed in.

Sharif, on the other hand, did exactly what his money manager told him to do. One day, when silver was still up there, his manager called and said they were getting out. Sharif traded out of all his contracts. A few weeks later the silver market collapsed.

Sharif generated several thousand dollars in commissions for the commodities broker and paid his money manager a modest fee, considering the total profits. My dentist friend generated close to a hundred thousand in commissions. And, as I said, when it was all said and done, the dentist had nothing and Sharif walked away with close to $4 million.

The moral here is that a professional money manager directing a commodities broker can be successful in moderate pyramiding. The reason, quite simply, is that he has the distance to be objective. He's working with your money, so you have the greed/fear motivations. He, on the other hand, has the distance to operate a plan/model.

This is not to say that the average person couldn't be successful with moderate pyramiding. It's only to say that I've never seen it happen. The average person very quickly deteriorates into a situation where he's driven by greed. He pyramids far too aggressively and then, when the market turns, he loses it all.

That's why I said at the beginning that all pyramids fail for the average investor. If you're going to be investing your own funds, use a reverse pyramid, as described, but do not try to pyramid. Your timing won't be perfect, you'll lose control, and the market will stomp on you.

On the other hand, if you're working with a professional and that professional at some point comes to you and says, "We're up substantially on your contract(s). Now, I think it's relatively safe to take a small portion of the profits and pyramid into a new contract," you're probably safe in taking his advice. His objectivity is going to make the difference.

STRATEGY 7—DON'T GET MARRIED TO A POSITION

No, this tip doesn't relate to love and sex (at least not directly). Rather, it refers to that expression that anyone who has ever invested in commodities has said at one time or another, "If only I had followed the system!"

Being married to a position is like marrying another person—it's for better or worse. Only with commodities, it's almost always for worse.

Let me illustrate what I mean when I talk about being married to a position in terms of my own personal life.

When I met my wife, my second wife, she, of course, knew that I was supposed to be this whiz kid with finances. However, she wouldn't invest a penny of her money into anything I suggested.

It's easier to change your attitude than it is to change the market.

B. R.

As an aside, she had been told by a fortune teller that she was going to be married five times and profit from the death of each husband. She'd already buried two husbands, each of whom had left her substantial sums of money.

I can't help but note that from her first marriage I did very well. I adopted her son, Tony, who has been a support in life and in business. From her second marriage I ultimately inherited the Roy McVicker Memorial desk and credenza set. It's a $50,000 (appraised value) piece of furniture, and since her second husband was a U.S. Congressman (Democrat), I can't help but wonder how he accumulated a $50,000 desk on $40,000 a year salary? But that's a story for a different book.

Her CPA (actually her dead husband's CPA) told her, "Mary, we don't want to invest with Bill. We don't want to invest with any money manager—it's too risky. We'll put all your money in CDs (certificates of deposit)."

My wife and I truly love each other; however, financially she was married to this position of sticking her money into CDs as advised by her CPA. It was her money, so naturally I didn't try to interfere. I did try to talk her out of it—to diversify, to try stocks, commodities, and real estate. But she was financially married to the CDs. She was convinced they were the only and the safest way to invest.

What I didn't know at the time was that the CPA, when he got her to sign the paperwork for the CDs, also put in there that he had the right to borrow against the CDs. He borrowed and borrowed and lost all the money! Ultimately, my wife got nothing, and the accountant went to prison.

My wife now believes in spreading her investments around. She is no longer married to CDs. (She also believes in investments that she can wear. She wears into the six figures in furs and in jewels because she likes to have things that no matter what, she knows she can get to them and they'll still be there.) By the way, if that fortune teller's prediction was correct, that she's going to marry five husbands and profit from the deaths of all of them, I've got the next one bamboozled—I've got trusts and corporations set up so that money goes where it belongs— to the kids. But that's another story.)

Marrying a position is like knowing—with the kind of certainty that comes only from God—that your investment is not only going to make you a lot of money, but also be safe. When you have that certainty, then you're married to a position. In commodities, it's also almost a sure bet that you're going to lose.

I once wrote an article in my newsletter on corn. It was a special situation, something that is unique and you can't count on, but when it happens, you better be there to take advantage of it.

Corn was around $1.80 a bushel. I had studied the fundamentals and the technicals, and I wrote, "I have never been so sure of anything in my life as I am that corn is going to go to $2.50." (That's a substantial move which could yield fantastic profits given the leverage of commodities.)

I remember what a good friend of mine, Joe, said. (I was carrying his account.) He called as soon as he read the newsletter and said, "I don't want anything to do with corn!"

Naturally I was surprised. I asked, "Joe, I'm dead sure. This is like shooting ducks in a barrel. Why don't you want to take advantage of it?"

I'll never forget his reply. He said, "Your certainty is why I don't want to get in. It's going to cost me too much money."

The only thing you can't learn quickly is experience.

B. R.

Too much money? At the time, I really didn't know what he meant. I was absolutely married to my position on corn. I put Joe aside and I went flying ahead with corn, and all my friends and accounts went along as well.

What happened? I was dead right. Corn went to $2.50. But I got killed along the way. My timing was wrong.

Corn moved to $1.90 and then took a twenty cent drop. It dropped to $1.70. A lot of people got out because of that. (A twenty cent drop was thousands of dollars per contract.) Those who got out weren't there when corn finally did get to $2.50.

That's just what Joe meant when he said it was going to be too expensive.

I was absolutely convinced that corn was going to make the big jump. So I stayed in there, married to my position. No matter what the market told me, no matter what people with common sense told me, I hung in there, losing a pile of money on that twenty cent drop.

If I hadn't been married to my position, I would have gotten out of corn as soon as any signs of weakness developed. But no, I was convinced.

The moral to this story is that the moment you marry a position, you give up your ability to make intelligent market decisions. And the moment that happens, you start losing money.

My solution for this problem is to hire a money manager. I currently do that. I pay him 6 percent a year plus 15 percent of the profits. (Believe me, there are plenty of profits.)

Yes, we talk all the time. Today, if I'm absolutely sure that corn is going to explode in price, if I'm convinced beyond a doubt, I'll suggest to him that he buy corn . . . and then I'll leave him alone. Will he buy corn? Maybe . . . and maybe not. *He's not married to the position.* He'll look at it objectively and make his decision. And I've learned enough through the bitter experience I've just recited to know that I'm better off living with his decision, even though I might be totally opposed to it.

This, of course, gets back to why you need a money manager or a broker to handle your commodities investing for you. If you can't afford these, in a later chapter I'll show you how you can set up a system so that you can be your own money manager, what I call your own "judiciary."

STRATEGY 8—FOLLOW GOLD

As I noted in an earlier chapter, gold is a barometer of economic health. More specifically, gold is a barometer of inflation. There has never been a time when inflation has gone up sharply that gold did not likewise increase in value.

It's important to understand precisely how this phenomenon works. In actuality, it is often the case that gold does not truly increase in value—rather, currencies decrease in value while gold retains its buying power.

Let's take the Mexican peso as an example. Between 1986 and 1988 the peso went from roughly 100 to the dollar to 1,000 to the dollar. That means that whereas before it took 100 pesos to buy a bottle of milk (worth roughly one American dollar), it later took 1,000 pesos to buy the same bottle of milk (which now cost roughly one and a quarter American dollars—the dollar was declining in value as well).

During that same period of time, the price of gold *in pesos* went from roughly 4,000 pesos an ounce to about 50,000 pesos an ounce. Do you see what's happening here?

From the perspective of pesos, the price of gold rose enormously. From the perspective of gold, the value of the peso declined enormously. Which perspective is correct? Both are!

If the mountain won't come to Mohammed, Mohammed will go to the mountain.

The Koran

The whole point is that gold retains its value while currencies, including both the Mexican peso and the American dollar, lose theirs.

Therefore, one way to tell when *significant* inflation is beginning is to watch the price of gold. Gold will signal the start of the next inflationary period.

Gold's Relevance to Commodities

As also noted earlier, commodities are likewise inflation sensitive. If we forget for a moment about fundamental (supply and demand) and technical (charting) price movements, there is another influence on the commodities market and that is, simply, inflation.

Commodities have roughly the same relationship to inflation as gold does. Consider that a bushel of soybeans may cost $5.00 in January. Now, let's just say that the economy of the United States really goes to pot and the United States has a 100 percent rate of inflation during the year. What could we reasonably expect that same bushel of soybeans to sell for *overlooking fundamental and technical* vagaries? The answer, quite predictably, is $10.

You see, soybeans are a commodity which has intrinsic value. Regardless of what's happening to currency, soybeans are going to be bought and sold and eaten. Assuming that the supply and demand factors remain constant and that there aren't any technical aberrations, the price of soybeans should fluctuate in inverse proportion to inflation, just as the price of gold should.

The problem with soybeans, however, is that we can never eliminate fundamental and technical factors. There may be a drought reducing the next crop or an especially wet period enhancing it. Thus, the price may be moving

That's the signal! That's the gold barometer telling you that it's time to plunge into commodities. The commodities themselves may not yet be responding, and you have to be careful not to be wiped out by bad timing. But gold's signal will be letting you know that a bull market in commodities is beginning, and that will be the quintessential time to get in.

STRATEGY 9—TAKE YOUR PROFITS

Earlier I wrote about the problems with taking your profits too early. I mentioned that "No one ever got hurt taking a profit" are the worst eight words ever spoken about commodities.

On the other hand, there is a time to take a profit. No commodity keeps going up (or down) forever in price. Eventually inflation ends or the supply catches up with the demand. Eventually it's time to cash in and move on.

How do you know when that time is?

You can have wisdom, you can have determination, you can even have capital, but you won't make a profit if you don't have a plan and stick to it.

B. R.

Hopefully, you've got a money manager handling that for you. As in the case of silver with Omar Sharif as noted earlier, the money manager says, "Get out, now!" and you take his very good advice.

But if you don't have a money manager or a broker handling your equity, then you have to make that decision yourself. How do you know when it's time to get out?

Technical systems can pick almost the exact turning point of the market. We'll see how some of these work in a later chapter, but for now, let's just say that computers are watching the market constantly and are trying to pick these turning points.

Far less accurate in terms of timing is watching the fundamentals. You can do this on your own without the aid of a computer. If you are watching an individual commodity, you can check for its supply and demand factors. These are reported daily in newspapers all over the world.

You can watch gold as a barometer of the market overall.

You can check for public announcements by officials. (Remember when the Secretary of the Treasury announced that the United States would let the dollar fall relative to other currencies—there are occasional signals such as that.)

But most important, you can keep to the discipline of your system, whatever it might be. Your system is going to have certain parameters. They may be money parameters—if your equity declines a certain amount, you're out. Never mind what seems to be happening in the marketplace, you take the profits you've made and run.

Your system may have price parameters. The price drops (or rises) by a certain percentage and you're history.

Your system may be based on sunspots. There's been an increase in sunspots for the past seven days, so you're right out of the market.

The point to be made here is that whatever your system, if it tells you to get out, take your profits and leave. The greatest danger comes from improvisation. You're making money hand over fist and suddenly your system says get out. "Why should I get out?" you're most likely to say. "I've just made $250,000. If I stay in the market another week I'll double that! No way am I getting out!"

Remember the dentist who lost all his profits on silver? Remember my own experiences in grain? Was it the reversal of direction in the price of silver (from $50 back down to $10) that caused him that loss? Was it the reversal in prices in grain that caused mine? Nope. It was lack of discipline.

As I exceeded mine, the dentist also exceeded the parameters of his system. There were certainly warning signals. Silver hovered at $50 an ounce for nearly six weeks before plunging. Any system would have been ringing red bells and sounding sirens given the volatility of the price rise (from $6 to $50) that a break was coming. Any money manager worth his salt would have said, "Get out, now!"

Always take money out of the market—never put it in.

B. R.

But our dentist wouldn't take his profits and run. Instead he stayed in there and lost them all.

Yes, you can get hurt by taking a profit too early. But you can also get hurt by failing to take a profit at all.

STRATEGY 10—DON'T VIEW COMMODITIES AS AN END ALL

This is really important, and those who understand it come away from commodities as wealthy individuals. Those who don't understand it keep playing commodities and never really get anywhere.

Commodities are a means to an end. If you trade commodities correctly, you can obtain an enormous amount of money very quickly. Because of their leverage, volatility, and liquidity, you can turn a few thousand dollars overnight into literally hundreds of thousands of dollars.

But then what do you do? Do you now play commodities for higher stakes? Whereas before you were buying one contract, do you now buy ten? Do you take your hundreds of thousands of dollars of profits and plow them back into commodities so you can make millions? And when you do, do you plow that back in so that you can make billions?

No! You don't do that at all—if you're smart.

Remember, the commodities market offers enormous leverage, and that's both its strong point and its weak point. To succeed in commodities investing, you want to always be taking advantage of that leverage. That means that you're going to always be a small player. Typically, a hundred thousand to half a million dollars is the average size of a "large player's" commodity account.

That's not much in the world of finance. In stocks it could be a million or ten million dollars.

Consider that a money manager in commodities who has $20 million under management, in my estimation, has all that he can handle. In stocks, money managers might be handling $500 million.

The point I'm making here is that while there is just as much money overall at risk in the commodities market as in the stock market, because of the leverage, there is only 10 percent (or less) as much money actually invested in stocks.

When you make a profit in commodities, unlike stocks, you don't plow it back in. Rather, you go back to the beginning with the same investment and start over.

Think of it this way—commodities are like a money making machine. When you make a profit, you don't get a bigger machine. You just run the machine a second time, and a third time, and so on. It keeps making you money on the same size of investment.

Two points should be made about this: First, there is a minimum size necessary for full diversification in commodities. As noted earlier, it is between $50,000 and $100,000. If you don't have that much money to start with, you will need to keep plowing your equity back until you run that kind of figure.

What to Do with Profits?

The second point to make has to do with profits. If you don't plow them back into commodities, what do you do with them? My suggestion is that you stick them into real estate.

> *"The thing about real estate is that they ain't makin any more of it!"*
>
> Will Rogers

Consider how the fortunes in this country have been made and held. I take as my example the Wrigley fortune from Chicago. How did Mr. Wrigley do it?

Do you think he did it making chewing gum? Do you think that everytime somebody put a penny in a vending machine, Mr. Wrigley made another million dollars?

Think again. The chewing gum industry, which he virtually created, was a money making machine for him. It allowed him to generate a significant cash flow. But, you can only sell so much gum. He couldn't keep plowing the money back in because he was limited in what he could sell.

So he bought real estate. The Wrigley family over decades, indeed over the better part of a century, acquired enormous real estate holdings. Those holdings increased in value over time—a very long time—so that their fortune became based on property, not gum. Gum was the money generator. But real estate was where that money went to grow and over a hundred years, to become one of the country's greatest fortunes. (If you doubt this, look around in your city. There are few big cities in this country that do not have, or did not once have, property owned by the Wrigley family.)

It's true for the Howard Hughes fortune, for the Vanderbilt fortune, for just about every fortune you can name in this country. They made money in oil or airplanes or chewing gum. But they did not look at their money machines as end alls. Rather they were the means to the end . . . which was real estate.

Let's do the same thing. But let's not get confused. Real estate is not the money machine. (That's not to say you can't make money in real estate. But you can make it faster in commodities.) Real estate is where you put the money you make with your money machine.

Let's all try to make the Forbes 500 list (500 richest people in America). Only we don't have an oil well or 500 oil wells. We don't own a factory manufacturing airplanes. We aren't as lucky as Donald Trump who slam dunks in real estate like no one else can.

But we still need a money machine. We still need a place to start. Why not start with commodities? Why not let commodities be our means to the end? Why not let commodities be our money machine?

7

CHARTING COMMODITY PRICES—PRO AND CON

It's really important that you understand the difference between fundamental and technical analysis. Fundamental analysis attempts to determine the trend of future prices in a commodity by watching the supply/demand ratio and other factors such as government influence (tariffs, taxes, embargoes, etc.) which affect prices. You can be a great fundamentalist by reading the financial papers and watching for those factors which influence a particular commodity.

But unless you're also a great technician, you will miss the big plays. The reason is that while fundamentalists can identify long-term trends, it takes a technician to pick the turning points when those trends start.

A technician watches prices—just prices. From those prices and from historical precedents regarding prices, the technician attempts to determine the beginnings of trends.

Technical analysis today is so advanced and so amazingly accurate that it is relied upon *almost exclusively* by a great many traders.

Even the market makes a mistake once in a while.

B. R.

Technical analysis, ultimately, is statistical. That is, it involves numbers—lots and lots of numbers. Since these numbers very quickly become cumbersome, very quickly in the development of technical analysis the numbers gave way to charts. While the numbers represent the raw data, the charts display the data in such a way that you and I can see possible trends at a glance.

Within the last 15 years, charts have become less important as computers have taken over. The computers examine the raw numbers and then, according to their programming, make buy/sell recommendations.

Nevertheless, from the human perspective, charts are easy to visualize and understand. In this chapter we are going to examine technical analysis, charts, and how computer commodity programs operate. I think it will be an eye-opener for you as you begin to see how the various systems work . . . and why they don't!

MOVING DAY AVERAGES

The goal of technical analysis is to identify the start or turning point in trends. The most simpleminded way of doing this is to just keep track of prices of a commodity over a period of time. You might, for example, record the closing prices of copper each day. (Closing prices are used partly as a convenience since that price is known whereas during the day the price can fluctuate significantly. Also, closing prices often most closely reflect the "true" current price for the commodity because when traders commit at the close, they know they won't be able to get in again until the following day.)

You might keep recording those closing prices for months (or even years), and you might note that the closing price each day is around 80 cents. Then, one day you notice that the price is beginning to move up. Plotting a graph you begin to notice that it's now closing in the 85 cent range. A month or two later it's closing in the 90 cent range. Your chart has shown you that an upward trend in price is occurring.

There is a problem, however. A simple day closing price chart will have a lot of ups and downs. One day it might close at 85 cents, a few days later at 90 cents, the following week at 80 cents, then a few weeks later back at 85 cents. Are you seeing a trend? Or are you just seeing the normal up and down fluctuations found in any market?

Hindsight is wonderful. You can go back to your chart and point out that, yes, there was a trend and it did start six months ago. Looking back it's easy to see.

Forecasts are like icebergs. They only tell you 10 percent of what's there. It's the 90 percent that you can't see that can kill you.

B. R.

However, looking forward is another matter. Knowing that a trend began six months ago is like knowing the winners at yesterday's daily double at the track. Everybody knows it and there aren't a whole lot of ways to make money on it. You need to know a trend *when it's just developing.*

This problem with charting was recognized earlier in this century when several individuals came up with the idea for a more refined chart—one that would more quickly and precisely indicate a trend. It was called a moving-day-average chart.

We've looked at moving day averages in earlier chapters. However, here we're going to see how they actually work to identify trends. You'll recall that to create a moving day average, you divided the number of days of the average by the closing prices of each day. Let's take a brief example.

We're following a commodity for three days. The closing prices for three consecutive days are $2.10, $2.05, and $2.15. For a three-day moving average, we add the closing prices and arrive at $6.30. Now we divide by the number of days in our moving average (3) and discover that the price for today is $2.10.

> day 1 $2.10
> day 2 $2.05
> day 3 $2.15
>   6.30/3 = $2.10

Tomorrow we repeat the calculation and so forth each day. Thus, each day we don't record the actual closing price but instead the moving average of closing prices.

What's the Effect of Following Moving Averages?

The effect is to smooth out the irregularities that exist in day-to-day trades. You might have a high day, a low day, and an in-between day. The three-day moving average just described smoothes them all out by taking the average of all three days.

Moving averages are typically computed for 3, 5, 10, 20, and 30 days. The longer the term, the smoother the chart. A 30-day moving price average chart is very smooth with trends clearly indicated. A three-day moving prices average chart is choppy, almost as choppy as a raw closing price chart.

However the advantage of a three-day chart over longer charts is that it signals a trend the soonest. The trouble is, because it's so choppy, you might miss the signal.

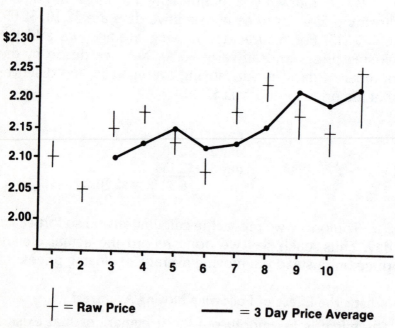

Three-day moving average.

The easiest way to clearly see a trend is to follow a long-term moving average chart. A 30-day price average will clearly identify a trend almost every time. By the time it's identified, however, everybody else may have already moved and it will be too late for you. Remember, what's easiest is not always best.

COMPETITION

The most important point I've been trying to get across in this book is that when you buy commodities, you don't buy in a vacuum. There are a lot of other guys and gals out there doing the same thing. And some of them are pretty darn smart. (If you weren't aware that I've been stressing that it's a competitive market, you need to reread some of the earlier chapters!)

Nothing's impossible if you think it isn't.

B. R.

The first fellow to invent moving day averages, a man named Donchian, made a killing in the market. The other traders couldn't figure how he always knew just when trends were starting. But as with gunpowder and the atomic bomb, there's no keeping secrets in this world. Eventually, his moving day average was out and everybody was using it. When everybody used it, its potency diminished. You simply couldn't get in at the beginning of a trend because everybody else was trying to get in at the same time. (This is an important point we'll return to shortly.)

What to do about it?

At first Donchian used ever shorter moving day averages. Instead of 30 or 25 days, he used 10 days and then 5 and even 3 days. The trouble is that, as we've seen, the shorter the number of days, the choppier the chart became and the less clearly it signaled. There had to be an answer.

Of course, there was.

CORRELATING MOVING DAY AVERAGES

The answer is to chart two averages, a long-term average and a short-term average, and then to plot them against each other. It's not hard nor all that complicated, although at this point a hand-held calculator or a computer might be helpful.

Here's how it works. We take, for example, a 20-day moving average and a five-day moving average. The 20-day average is our long-term indicator. The five-day average is our short-term indicator.

Now, everytime the five-day average breaks out over the 20-day average, we've got an uptrend indication. Anytime it breaks down, we've got a downtrend indication.

Why? Think it through. The 20-day average is mellowing out prices over 20 days. But the five-day average is showing prices over the *last five days*. Hence, when the prices of the last five days differ sharply from the prices of the previous 20 days, you've got a good indication of a trend.

Thus, by correlating moving day averages, short against long, very quickly we can get an easy-to-read and surprisingly accurate indication of the market.

The first definitive study of commodity trading over a 25-year period of time examined the use of five-day moving averages correlated against 20-day moving averages. The result? You could have put your money manager away and just used your calculator to sweep in the profits. You could have taken $2,000 easily up to well over a million dollars, probably something closer to three million. That's not to say you would never have lost money. You would have lost in one out of four or five years. The rest of the time it was a gravy train.

Those who did it back in 1974 and 1975 when the stock market fell through the floor were making fortunes. It was then that computer trading first was examined and when the first sophisticated computer programs for trading commodities came into existence. All that they basically did was to correlate moving day averages and send out the signal when the short average broke through the long average. Yet that was enough to make a good many fortunes.

EXPONENTIAL MOVING DAY AVERAGES

As before, competition wiped out the advantage. When only a few people knew how to correlate moving day averages, it was easy to make a bundle. But when every brokerage house and broker in the country was following moving day averages, you couldn't get in early enough. When the signal went out, it was out to everyone and they all jumped in at the same time. Consequently, to beat the competition, the system was refined.

The next version did require computers and very sophisticated programs. The logic that was devised was something like this.

I and a very few other people began to say, "I'm not trying to reinvent moving day averages. I'm not trying to reinvent the correlation of two moving averages. All I'm trying to do is to push this statistical system to its limit. I want to refine it to the point where I get the signal one day, or one hour, or even one minute before the next guy. That small an edge in the volatile and computerized marketplace of today can be enough to make my fortune."

Seek and ye shall find—but will you find that which you seek?

B. R.

The answer was exponential moving day averages. In an exponential system, you say that, yes we're going to relate five-day moving averages to 20-day averages or whatever. But we're going to recognize the movement of time as a factor. In the five-day averages, while we have five days, not each of those days is as important as the others. In fact the last day, today, is the most important because it is the latest indicator of prices. Yesterday was the second most important, the day before that the third most important, and so forth.

In other words, in an exponential system, we assign different weights to different days. The most recent days count the most.

Of course, the question now becomes, how do we know how much weight to assign each day? There are two answers. The simplest way is to arbitrarily assign weights to different days. In a 10-day system, today is worth 1.0, yesterday .9, the day before .8 and so forth. For each day further back in time I go, I reduce its importance by 10 percent.

The more effective method is to compare prices *historically*. Go back three years, five years, ten years or more and plug in the system. See how it would have performed as a trend signaler given different historical circumstances for each commodity. From that, correlate the proper weights to give each day. This can and has been done by computer.

Only now, there's wide divergence. No two exponential systems are exactly the same. Every system assigns different weights for different days of the moving average. Thus, not all the signals kick in at the same time. Some are earlier and some are later. And those that are earlier are often later the next time . . . depending on the circumstances.

THE CHART PATTERNS

Thus far we have been, in effect, simplifying the way the systems actually operate. (You think it hasn't been simple thus far? You haven't seen anything yet!)

We have been assuming that all that has to happen is for a shorter-term average to break through a longer-term average to signal a buy or sell order. In actual fact, just breaking through may not be enough. There are certain patterns that have been identified historically which indicate trends, and some of these patterns are statistically more reliable than others.

*The trouble is that by the time I learn what's happening,
the market has already discounted the news!*

Beginning trader

The computer systems have these patterns programmed into them. For simplicity, however, I have drawn them here as a real person, not a computer, would see them. Please keep in mind that these patterns are used all the time for technical analysis by unbelievably fast computerized trading systems. By the time you might identify any one of these trends, the computer has already seen it and signaled the broker to make the trade.

Even so, they are of value as we'll see shortly.

Uptrend

The prices move upward. Note, for it to be a true uptrend, both the tops and bottoms of the prices must trend upwards.

Downtrend

It's easy to see. The prices move downward. Note that in order for it to be a real downtrend, both tops and bottoms have to move down.

Head and Shoulders

The "head and shoulder" pattern is one of the most reliable. My own guess is that it's 70 percent reliable.

This pattern is easily recognizable since the name is so descriptive. Basically, if prices break out to the high side, above the head and shoulders, you've got a major price increase trend. If prices break to the down side, you've got a major price decline. You should be so lucky as to get a "head and shoulders" pattern a couple of times in

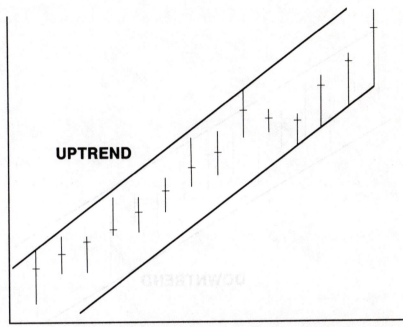

In an uptrend, both tops and bottoms of prices move upward.

a row. If that happens and you take advantage of it, you'll be rich very quickly.

Rounded Top and Rounded Bottom

In this pattern the prices of a commodity just roll over a top or a bottom. If on the top, it's an indication of a coming downtrend. If on the bottom, an indication of an uptrend. The size of the "saucer" or the rounded area is often an indication of the extent of the coming price advance or decline. A very large saucer indicates a major trend. A small saucer indicates a small trend.

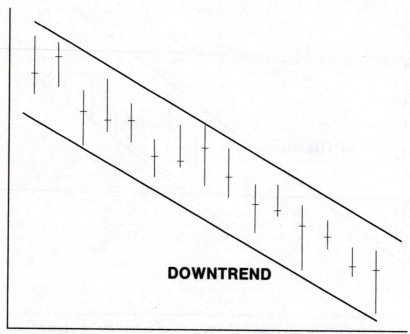

DOWNTREND

Tops and bottoms of prices move downward in a down trend.

Double Tops or Bottoms

These signal the end of a trend. Since the end of one trend may be the start of a new trend in the opposite direction, this can be very helpful. Think of a double top or bottom as someone who is trying to pierce a barrier. They try once, the first top or bottom. They try a second time. Then they give up.

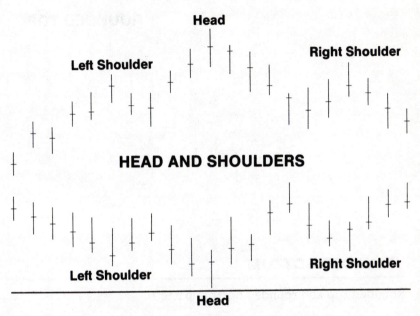

Head and shoulders pattern (upside and downside).

The inability to pierce a price range is what gives the double top/bottom so much signaling power. It indicates that there is enormous force in the other price direction just waiting to be unleashed.

Once in a great while there will be a triple top or bottom. It's an almost certain indicator of a coming reversal.

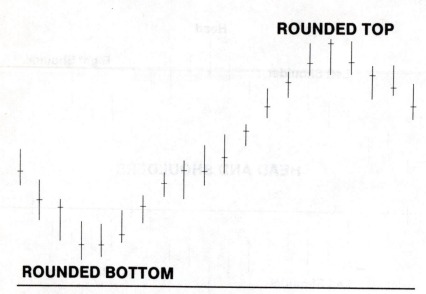

ROUNDED TOP

ROUNDED BOTTOM

Rounded top and rounded bottom pattern.

Trend Gaps

While in the other charts it is possible to watch only closing prices, for this chart it is necessary to watch the price range during an entire day. Gaps are price ranges in which the market does not trade. For example, on a particular day or group of days the price jumps up or down. This could be in the form of limit moves or it could be simply price hikes. All that it means is that on day two, the price traded was not the same as on day one.

For example, on Wednesday the market trades in a range of $2.03 to $2.11. On Thursday the market trades in a range of $2.18 to $2.31. In between was the range of $2.12 to $2.17 that the market never touched. This is called a gap.

DOUBLE TOP

Double top (or double bottom) pattern.

When the gap occurs in the midst of steady trading with no discernible trends, it is considered an aberration or a "common gap" and is given no particular significance.

When a gap occurs at the start of a major trend, it is called a "breakaway gap" and often signals later more dramatic moves to follow.

When a gap occurs after a trend has been in effect for some time, it is called a "runaway gap." It may be signaling that the trend still has plenty of steam left in it . . . that there are many more price movements to come.

Finally, when a gap occurs after there has been a major move followed by a period of steadily higher or lower prices, it is called an "exhaustion gap." It may signal the end of the trend and a coming reversal in prices.

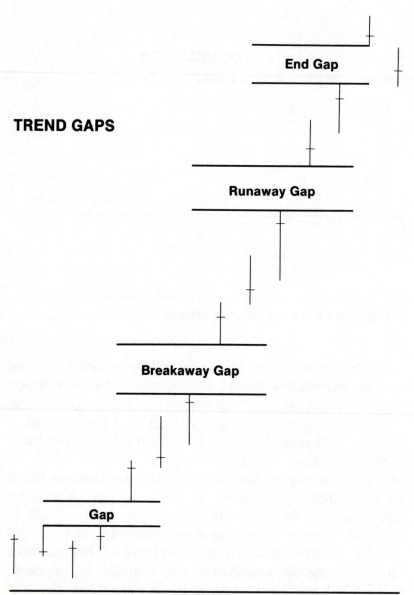

TREND GAPS

End Gap

Runaway Gap

Breakaway Gap

Gap

Trend gaps are price ranges in which the market does not trade—
the price jumps up or down.

Gapping patterns are found almost anytime in the market. The trick is to associate them with major trends in one direction or another.

CYCLES—FACTORING FUNDAMENTALS INTO TECHNICAL ANALYSIS

Finally, there is the well-known phenomena that commodities move in cycles. This is getting as close to a fundamental analysis as a technical analysis gets.

It is still statistical. From the technician's viewpoint, the reasons for the cycle are irrelevant. What counts is that there is a cycle at all.

What are cycles? Cycles are repetitions of price movements on a yearly or other basis. For example, it's fairly well known that housing prices slump in December and bounce back in June and July. The reason may be that in December no one wants to house hunt while in the summer, the kids are out of school and it's the ideal time to look. Whatever the reason, historically it's been shown that housing prices fluctuate annually in this fashion.

It works for commodities just like it does for houses, as long as there is a historical repetition. For example, there are well known seven-year cycles associated with cattle breeding. There are two- and three-year cycles associated with drought and grains. And so forth.

Once you know the cycle, you can factor it into your system. It's the second year after a drought, and farmers are plowing to beat the band so they can take advantage of the high prices the drought brought. Only now, the prices drop because of the oversupply. You can program that right in. You don't even need to know the current prices to understand that it's going to happen! You can also plot it on a chart, actually in advance of the occurrence.

THE ULTIMATE PROBLEM WITH CHARTING (TECHNICAL ANALYSIS)

So where's the rub? I've just given you the golden key to making money in commodities. By using technical analysis with a computer (or, if you're quick, a hand-held calculator and charts), you can move right in there with the champs. You can determine price trends almost as they happen. You can go on to make your fortune.

Indeed you can!

However, before you start spending all that money you're going to make, consider the following. As I mentioned earlier in this book, the computer systems— *all the computer systems—are right only 40 percent of the time.*

> *Always plan as though you're a general fighting a war.*
>
> B. R.

Think about it. Even with the best sophistication, all the systems can do is to signal true trends less then half the time. The other 60 percent it's just an aberration, a momentary flash in the pan, a couple of speculators banging and setting the market off in a false move.

What happens then? Why, all of us who are watching the computers and the trends and are charting jump in. We wait to ride the crest of the wave to profit. Only as soon as it becomes apparent that the signal was wrong, we bail out.

Hence, today's market is filled with false moves. The signal goes out. Thousands and thousands of people buy pork bellies. The price begins to move up.

You saw the signal too with your charting on your computer. Now you see the price beginning to move, so you jump in too. Only it's not really a trend. It's just all of us jumping in causing a blip in prices. When the market doesn't go anywhere after a few hours or days, we're all out. And if you're not out, you've lost a grand or two . . . on a false signal.

Such are the treacheries of commodity trading today.

PROFITING FROM CHARTS

Even so, the technical analysis, the charts, are correct 40 percent of the time. And as we saw in earlier chapters, if you hit those 40 percent and let your money ride, you'll be sitting on easy street in a very short time.

The truth is that ultimately technical analysis works. Ultimately charts and computers work. Ultimately they can make your fortune for you.

You can be a dumb ox and still look like a wise owl in the commodities field if you follow technical analysis and charts—and if, by the way, you happen to be loaded with money.

You see, in today's market, everyone who is sophisticated knows about technical analysis, charts, and computer systems. Only not everyone wins. John Brown may be following the XYZ computer system and be making $25 thousand a month. Susy Smith may be following the same system and be losing that amount.

Why? It's simple, Here's my gift to you, the reader. All the systems work. They are all capable of making money for you. Even the simple moving day average works.

The thing to remember, however, is that *they are always throwing out signals*. They never stop signaling. The truth of today's marketplace is that computer systems and the charts don't run out of signals, investor accounts run out of money.

You and I run out of either emotional money (we can't make the next trade) or physical money. Following the signals is like getting on a bucking bronco. You know that if you stick on long enough, you'll hear the bell and have a winning ride.

But in the meantime, all you can think about is how that bronc is bucking and twisting and how you hurt in places you never knew existed before. Long before the end of the ride, most investors jump (not fall, but jump) off.

HOW TO MAKE IT WORK FOR YOU

How do you resolve the dilemma? How do you use the information that the charts and computer systems via technical analysis give you with the emotionally and financially taxing ride they produce? There are two answers.

If you've got enough funds, you hire a money manager. You let him ride the bronc for you. You just take the credit at the end of the ride.

When you're tired, sleep. When you're rested, trade.

H. K.

Your money manager takes all the abuse—which he's capable of handling because, after all, it's not his money. All that you have to do is to pick the money manager who has a good system and who is truly capable of managing money successfully. (We'll have a whole lot more to say about this in later chapters.)

You can do this by sticking $50,000 to $100,000 with the manager—or by pooling your money with others as described earlier.

The second method is for the person who only has $2,000 or $3,000 to invest. What do you do?

My suggestion is that, yes, you do follow the charts as shown in this chapter. In fact, make your own charts. It's easy and only takes a few minutes a day.

But in addition, follow those fundamentals. You probably won't be able to follow all the commodities, so pick out three or five and follow those religiously. Check the papers each day for information on supply and demand. Watch out for any kind of government interference in the market (embargoes, taxes, supports, etc.) that might also affect prices.

And finally, once or twice a year when the fundamental signals and the technical signals all say to make a move, do it. Jump into the market and take your chance. You may only be able to open one contract for one commodity. But, if you hit it right, that's all you'll need! You'll be able to ride it up for a significant profit.

Now take that profit, if it's enough, and put it with a money manager. Don't make the mistake of believing in your own infallibility. Don't think you can keep repeating. *Don't get married to the charts.* Step one is to do it in a special situation. Step two is to take the profits and find that money manager.

CHARTING

That's what you need to know about charts. They are good, but they are less than 50 percent reliable. They operate just like the computer systems.

Use them wisely.

8

WHY YOU NEED
A MONEY
MANAGER

*I never got something for nothing. But that didn't stop me
from trying.*

W. C. Fields

You need a money manager, period.

In a hot market or when a commodity makes a major
move, two players can be right on top of the situation.
One player walks away with a fortune, the other is lucky
not to lose money. What's the difference between them?
The one who made it had a money manager, the one who
lost, didn't.

A money manager is not a commodities broker. A
commodities broker executes orders for you. You tell your
broker to buy wheat and he buys. He suggests you sell
copper and you think it's a pretty good idea, so you say
go ahead. He sells.

The broker doesn't manage your money. He spends
it.

A money manager is one step removed from a commodities broker. The money manager has a computerized system that he follows rigorously. He follows the market and decides when to be in and when to be out and which commodities to trade.

(It's important to understand that in most cases when you hire a money manager what you're really hiring is a computer system. The money manager trades in a matrix, a group of commodities. The computer follows the matrix and throws out buy or sell signals when it identifies trends. The person involved is only required to have the discipline to follow the signals—once, of course, the system has been programmed.)

You don't directly give your money to the money manager. Rather, you sign an agreement with him, typically a power of attorney (see the next chapter). This allows him to invest your money in your stead. Now, instead of you calling up your broker and saying, "Buy soybeans, sell yen," your asset manager makes the call and places the order.

It's your money, your profits and your losses. The difference? You don't make the decisions. The money manager does.

THE TROUBLE WITH PASSION

Why would any reasonable person want to give up control of his or her money? Why give up control of what to invest in and when?

The answer is both simple and complex. The simple answer is that the money manager, presumably, knows more than you do; hence he or she has a better chance of success.

Tips are like merchants who sell cheap goods—their value is suspect.

B. R.

The trouble is that the simple answer isn't necessarily true. After all, if you study the market, both fundamentally and technically as described in the previous chapters, you should be able to pick those two or three major moves each year. You should be able to manage your own money quite successfully.

You can do well in the market, if you work at it, from an intellectual perspective. The problem here isn't so much a matter of knowledge, however, as one of emotion. That's the complex answer.

As we saw in earlier chapters, the person who manages his or her own account is subject to the passions of investing. Remember the dentist in the silver market? He was trading in and out and around and ended up with nothing. The moral there was "don't pyramid." However, the story has another application. It was, after all, that dentist's own passion for the market that kept him pyramiding and ultimately cost him his profits.

As I've noted elsewhere in the book, when you direct your trades, eventually you become so involved in what you're doing (remember the section on marrying a position) that you finally make the wrong decision. Intellectually, you may know what to do. But, emotionally you can't come up with any more money or make the next trade or stick with the position. Your passion kills you.

That's why you need a money manager. They are passionless. After all, it's not their money. They operate mechanically. The moment a money manager becomes emotionally involved in an account's money, that's the time to get out.

YOUR FINANCIAL GOVERNMENT

A good way to think about this is in terms of a financial government. Your financial government is similar to the American political system. It has three branches: executive, judicial and legislative.

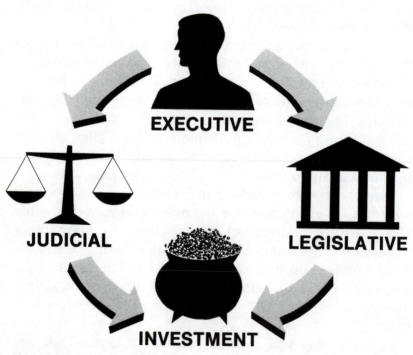

Your financial government.

Executive

Here's the branch of your financial government where the decisions are made. You decide to buy gold or to sell orange juice. At that point when you actually make the decision to trade, you're using your executive talents.

Legislative

This is the part of your financial government that makes the rules. Here you decide on what trading system to use. You study the market and analyze it fundamentally and technically. You prepare a trading plan.

> *Nothing's worth not being able to sleep at night.*
>
> Napoleon

Why You Need a Judicial Branch

Now, most of us only have two branches of government. We use the legislative branch to make the trading rules and the executive branch to execute them. We get into the market and we're doing fine—until we start winning or losing.

We buy British pounds (why, I don't know, but perhaps pounds are doing well this month). We buy them at $1.50 (each pound is worth $1.50 in U.S. currency). Our studying has convinced us that the pounds are going to make a major move upward.

Almost immediately, the pound starts going up in value relative to the dollars. Within a week it's at $1.55. By the end of a month it's up to $1.69. We've made a few bucks and we're feeling pretty cocky. After all, we caught the market. Our analysis tells us that this is just the beginning. All we have to do is sit tight and ride for the profits.

Only now something unexpected happens. The pound begins to fall in value. From $1.69, it drops to $1.64. Since our contract was for 25,000 pounds, each cent the pound moves is worth $250. When it went from $1.69 down to $1.64, it dropped six cents or $1,250.

We lost $1,250! The thought both energizes and paralyzes us. If we had just sold a week earlier, we wouldn't have lost that money. What fools we are!

At this point the legislative breaks into our executive self-criticism and says, "Hey, remember the *plan*. We're waiting for the pound to make a big move. Sure, it dropped a few cents, but it's just a temporary setback on the way to $2.00."

We try to calm ourselves and wait. Over the next few weeks, the pound drops more and more until it's at $1.56, just one cent over where we got into the market.

"What a fool you are," our executive is telling us. "Why did you listen to legislative? If you had sold back when it was still $1.64, you would have made $2,250 profit. Now your profits are down to just $250. And the way the market is going, by tomorrow, you'll be in the hole!"

"But the plan . . ." screams the legislative.

Screw the plan, you tell yourself. Let's get out with at least cab fair. You call your broker and sell.

Two days later, the pound turns around again and never stops until it hits $1.90. If you had stayed in the market just another few days, you would have made a $10,000 profit instead of a $250 one.

Of course, you're going to kick yourself. But are you going to really understand what happened? Do you really see why you lost out?

Never cry over spilt milk.

Anonymous

The answer is that there was no buffer between the legislative and the executive branches. The rules were made and they were executed. But, when the market started moving, the passion of the executive lost sight of the rules. Plain and simple, the executive panicked.

Something very similar to this, I suspect, could happen in our own political form of government if there was only Congress and the President. Fortunately, there's that other branch of government, the Supreme Court.

The judicial branch examines the laws made by the legislative and determines their constitutionality. Or, to put it another way, determines if they'll work. It also examines the actions of the executive branch and determines if they are appropriate. The judicial branch is the buffer which brings harmony and success to our political system.

Similarly, we need a judicial branch of our financial government. We need a Supreme Court. If we have it, then when the market plays a trick on us, the judicial can stand back and say, "Were the rules of the legislative branch appropriate? Is there really justification for holding our position and waiting for a major market move?"

At the same time the judicial can also examine the executive and say, "Don't panic. We need to be thoughtful, not emotional."

In other words, the judicial branch of our financial government is passionless. (Remember the symbol of justice is *blind*.) It examines the facts and makes its decision.

If we had had a judicial branch of our financial government operating when we invested in British pounds, it would have stood back and looked at the legislative actions. It would have judged the question of whether or not the pound was in a major move and whether or not this decline was simply a temporary setback. Presumably, it would have concluded that it was a setback and kept us in the market.

You see, the judicial wouldn't worry about losing $1,250 or $2,250 dollars. It would keep its eye on the distant goal of making $10,000.

The Judicial Branch

Who is the judicial branch of government? Of course, it's the money manager.

The money manager operates on a system and is paid for his or her discipline. That discipline forms the judicial branch of your financial government. You're panicking because the pound is down. But the money manager is looking at it dispassionately and saying, "We'll keep our position."

What are you going to do? Overrule your money manager? If you do that, why did you get him in the first place?

What you do is take his advice . . . and make the $10,000 profit that you, on your own, would lose.

That's why you need a money manager.

IF YOU CAN'T AFFORD A MONEY MANAGER

What if you're just starting out and you can't afford a money manager? How do you manage?

There is no easy answer. But there is an answer. The first thing you do is to realize that you have three branches to your financial government. Knowledge is power in this case.

Once you understand that, each time there is a crisis, you have to make a conscious effort to change hats. When the British pound drops, you stop being the executive. You take off your crown and put on your judicial robes.

Forget your first loss. Forget your first profit even sooner.

B. R.

Stand back. Forget about what you've lost. (After all, it is just fantasy money.) Examine the parameters of your system. Are you within the parameters? If so, are you prepared to abandon the system? If not, then you'll stick with your position (in this case).

No, being your own judiciary is not easy, not easy at all. But at least if you once see what you have to do, you've got a leg up on doing it. And if you do it well only a few times, you'll move up to be in position to afford your own money manager.

THE TROUBLE WITH MONEY MANAGERS

Thus far we've been speaking of money managers as if they were the end-all God-send to our problems. If that were the case, then everyone would have a money manager and be filthy rich. Neither is the case. There are problems with money managers.

Passion is not usually one of the problems. Money managers, as we've seen, tend to be automatons; they are disciplined to follow their computer systems.

The real problem has to do with specialization. There are many, many money managers out there, and they all have different approaches. But regardless of what approach they take, they are all specialists.

A specialist is one who learns more and more about less and less until he knows everything about nothing. A generalist is one who learns less and less about more and more until he knows nothing about everything.

B. R.

This applies to money managers and their systems. They believe that their system is the only way to trade, even though there are thousands and thousands of other money managers who believe that some other system is the only way to trade. They tend to be ivory tower thinkers, and that is their weakness.

As a result, they tend not to be people-oriented. If you want to discuss the technical aspects of their trading system with them, they'll wear you out with their comments. On the other hand, if you want to discuss the pros and cons of giving them control of your money, you won't get much out of them. Their attitude, frequently, is that, "of course you should put your money with me. It's the only rational thing to do and you, as a rational being, should see that."

That's pretty hard to swallow when it's your hard-earned $100,000. You want a bit more than just a machine. You want to be cajoled and convinced. Unfortunately, most money managers are not much into personal relations, and they'd just as soon that you leave it as take it.

What this means to you is that frequently you're going to have to go the extra mile with the money manager, even though it's your money and he's working for you.

When your broker suggests a money manager (in the next chapter we'll see how to get brokers to do this for you), you'll have to make the introductions and carry the ball. Just remember, you don't need a money manager to be a bosom buddy . . . just to make money for you.

9

HOW TO
FIND THE
RIGHT MONEY
MANAGER

Whatever the mind of man can conceive, he can achieve.
Napoleon Hill

There are two big problems with commodities money managers:

Problem #1—Your broker can't afford to direct you to a money manager. He's in a vicious cycle of continually trying to open accounts and milk the accounts he has for commissions.

As a result, you're not going to get a broker to very easily introduce you to a money manager. However, there are a lot of investors who do trade with money managers, and in order to survive, brokers become knowledgeable about money managers. Thus, it becomes a matter of approach. If you go to a broker and say, "Let's trade on our own or let's hire a money manager," the broker will always opt to trade "on our own" (which means his commissions, your equity).

On the other hand, if you say, "Let's hire a money manager or I'll go elsewhere," the broker may suddenly remember a money manager. The trouble is, this in itself isn't a great solution. Brokers only tend to remember money managers who generate good commissions for them. Yes, they'll look for a good enough record to entice you. But let's say we have money manager A who does a lot of trades generating lots of commissions and has a fair record and money manager B who does a few trades generating few commissions but who has an outstanding record. Now, who do you think your broker will recommend to you?

We'll have more to say about how to get around this problem later in this chapter.

Problem #2—By the time you find a money manager on your own, it's too late. The rule I have in using money managers in commodities is that *success breeds failure, not success.* This means that as the money end of management increases (as the manager gets more money under management), the ability to live up to past performance decreases. The corollary to this rule is that there are no real exceptions.

Look at any firm that handles money as a manager. Look at the funds that have done the best and you'll find that after they have done extremely well, they attract a great deal of money. (Everyone chases the "hot hand.") As more and more money comes in, the ability to live up to those exciting past performances goes down. Any honest firm will tell you that.

DECLINING PERFORMANCE

Why? Why does performance decrease as money under management increases?

In stocks, a money manager can handle a billion dollars. He can do it without any problems. But in commodities, a money manager is only going to be able to handle $10 million, maybe $20 million . . . certainly no more.

The reason has to do with leverage, regulations, and motivation. Let's look at each:

The Problems of Leverage

Remember, in commodities you normally are working with a leverage factor of 10 to 1. Rounded out, that means that a money manager who has $20 million in commodities under management is roughly equivalent to a stock manager who has $200 million under management. The leverage does it.

The more money you use, the harder it is to make more money in commodities.

B. R.

In addition, also remember that chances are that the commodities money manager only has a small percentage of that money in play in the market at any given time. He may have only 10 or 15 percent in play and may be holding back the rest. That again increases the leverage by another factor of 10 so that the $20 million commodities manager may, in fact, be roughly equivalent to a $2 billion stock manager.

Leverage means that a small amount of money in commodities involves an enormous responsibility and challenge. Thus as the money manager acquires more and more accounts, his ability to meet that responsibility and challenge gets spread thinner and thinner.

Government Regulation

Another factor is government regulation. A commodities money manager is regulated. He can only accumulate so many contracts of a commodity before he's considered to be exercising a negative effect on the market and has to stop. There are strict limits on the number of accounts a broker can carry (as well as how many a client can carry).

Unfortunately, a money manager is considered one account. All of his accounts are considered one account, so he has to live within a tight rein. Generally, that's about $20 million under management.

Finally There's Motivation

To understand motivation, it's helpful to consider the "life cycle" of a money manager. A typical manager starts out small. He has a number of accounts, and maybe he has a million dollars under management. His fees are typically six percent a year plus 15 percent of the profits. (Profit incentive fees are standard in the industry. They vary from 20 percent straight profits to 12 percent straight fees. But a 6/15 split is most common. In my opinion the cheapest way to go is to take the straight fees. Profit participation is not a smart play with commodities money managers as we'll see.)

That means he's taking in $60,000 a year plus his profit participation. Well, if he's a money manager, he's got an office, a secretary, a computer system, and a telephone with a lot of lines. He's doing some wholesaling, and I guarantee you he's spending that full $60,000 a year on his business. So what does he live off of?

He lives off that 15 percent profit participation. He has got to make money for his clients in order for him to survive. He's lean and hungry and he's making every kind of successful trade there is. He knows that if he blows even one or two trades, he'll lose an account he can't afford to lose.

So he's successful. And success attracts more money. Other accounts come to him and ask him to take them on. They want him to do for them what he's done for his existing accounts. He matures into a middle-aged money manager (in terms of the life cycle of money managers).

Pretty soon he doubles the $1 million to $2 million, then $4 million and eventually he's got $10 million under account.

Now, when he only had $1 million under account, his fees brought in $60,000. Now with $10 million under account, they bring in $600,000. When he had $1 million, his fees barely covered his operating expenses. Now they cover not only his operating expenses, but leave a big chunk to live on. When he had only $1 million under account, he had to make that 15 percent participating profit or he couldn't survive. With $10 million under account, if he makes it, great. If he doesn't, well, he's always got that $600,000 to fall back on.

When a money manager's got $1 million under account, he's praying to God he makes you money. When he's got

$10 million under account, he's praying to God he doesn't lose your money. There's a big difference.

B. R.

Ultimately, what it all means is that the more money under management, the less able the manager is to handle it, the more problems with government regulations, and the less motivation to make profits. As a result, the performance of managers declines as the money in accounts goes up.

MAKING YOUR CHOICE

There are a lot of studies which suggest that the way to pick a money manager is to check his volatility, the peaks and valleys of the trading he does in a month or other period, as well as to check his success. The trouble is that all those studies are useless because by the time you normally find the money manager, his motivation has changed. By the time you learn about his successes, his motivation is to keep what he's got, not to make you money.

Is it hopeless then?

No, not at all. It's just . . . challenging. On the one hand you have to coerce your broker into introducing you to a money manager who is going to make you money. On the other hand, you have to get to him before he's grown so fat and satisfied that he won't perform as well as he did in the past.

Mistakes in Picking Money Managers

All right, you're looking for the lean and hungry guy. You've gotten your broker to recommend a few (or more than a few) commodities money managers. Who do you pick?

Why, if you were like me when I first started out, you picked the guy who was obviously making the most money. That translated into the guy with the most lavish life style.

I had made some $600,000 in commodities in about 18 months on my own, and because of my losses in grains (remember, when I inadvertently was placed into contracts that ran me way up over a million and then hung onto them instead of closing and ran them back down), I was looking for a manager, my first manager. I got recommendations from people I knew in the field, and after checking several out, I ended up being fascinated by this one individual. He lived out in California, so I went to see him.

Buying a Reputation

He had a big mansion in Beverly Hills, he drove a Rolls Royce, he had a lovely wife, several children, and an obviously big business. Finally, he had been recommended by a man whose name was on the front door of a brokerage firm. I was hooked before I even entered his house.

> *There's never been a horse that couldn't be rode; there's never been a rider that couldn't be throwed.*
>
> Cowboy lament

Nonetheless, I asked him about his parameters. Remember, at this time I have something under $600,000 left, and I want to live off of it until I can figure out what to do with the rest of my life. I want him to make money, but more than that, I don't want him to lose it. As far as I'm concerned, this capital is totally irreplaceable.

So we went over his system. He was a fast trader. He went in and out of markets all the time. (It was no wonder that brokers liked him and he came highly recommended—remember the trap we just discussed?)

However, it seemed that his system worked well. He showed me the largest draw-down (loss of capital) that he had ever had in one month. It was 5 percent. That was outstanding, even brilliant. (You can't do that good in the stock or bond market!)

His average monthly profit on all his accounts was a staggering 8 percent. (That's *monthly* folks, not annually.)

So I hired him. But I watched him closely.

Within six weeks he doubled my money. I was very, very happy. I paid him 25 percent of the profits (no fee). And I let him trade without my watching him. (Watching is nerve wracking. I had been watching him every day and it was almost as bad as trading the market myself. Besides, he had more than lived up to the performance I expected. He had gotten off to one whale of a start.)

I called him on the phone and we made an agreement. We agreed that he would continue the account at $600,000 and not touch the profits. And feeling like the chief rooster in the barn, I went off traveling. I had discovered the legendary money tree. I was off in Europe, and my money manager was making me rich in America.

When I came back several months later, I was appalled. He had lost *80 percent* of my account. Of the $600,000, only $120,000 was left. Needless to say I was absolutely furious. This clown had taken me all the way down while I was out of town.

What he did while I was gone was decide to make a living off my account. He traded and traded until the equity was down. Then he tried to recoup by going for broke—he put all the money in one trade . . . and that trade went against him.

It was inexcusable. We had agreed on a system he would use, the parameters of which were clearly defined. Never had I agreed to an all or nothing trade. That was preposterous.

So I looked into suing him. Now, I'm not a proponent of lawsuits. I'm in the financial business, and there is no malpractice insurance for a financial asset manager like myself. So you can understand why I don't like lawsuits.

Nonetheless, I had been done in and I wanted revenge . . . or at least a small piece of this guy's hide.

Never beat a dead horse.

Will Rogers

So I had my attorneys prepare to go to court. First, however, I decided to investigate this money manager who had been recommended to me. There's an old rule that says, "Never sue if a guy doesn't have the dough." I wanted to verify that he had as much money as he appeared to have. I even went so far as to hire a private detective to check it out.

What did I find? His house in Beverly Hills was rented. He didn't own it. His Rolls Royce was rented. He didn't own it. Everything he had (maybe even his wife and kids!) were rented, all part of a very elaborate front. If I sued him and won, I would probably just have to stand in line.

So I didn't sue.

At this point I was very disillusioned. I had made money fast twice now, in big numbers . . . and had seen it disappear equally as fast. I was beginning to wonder if there was any validity in being in commodities. I was actually thinking of sticking what I had left in Treasury bonds.

At about this time, I was invited into one of the biggest brokerage houses for a meeting. I was asked, "Bill, aren't you tired of sitting on your rear end?"

I replied, "I'm more than tired of it. I'm beginning to think I can't afford it!"

I was asked to work for them and ultimately I did, as senior vice-president and at a hefty salary well into six figures. And in so doing I learned a few more lessons, one of which was now emblazoned in gold letters on my mind—never buy a reputation.

I also learned to check out the money manager before I hand him my money, not afterward.

And finally I learned to put the trading parameters in writing and to keep watch over the money manager (or to hire an asset manager, such as I now am) to watch over the various money managers working for you.

THE RIGHT WAY TO HIRE A MONEY MANAGER

We've seen the wrong way to hire a money manager (as I said, I've made all the mistakes). Now, let's look at the right way.

1. Get His Disclosure Document

Today a money manager must provide you with a disclosure document. In it are all the pertinent facts about the money manager. It lists how well he's done in the past. It goes without saying that he should have a track record going back six to ten years.

When most people look at a disclosure document, they quickly check to see how much money they would have made if they had used this guy. They look to see profits and gains.

2. Check the Draw-Downs

Looking at profits is baloney. Anybody who trades commodities regularly is going to show some spectacular profits. What really counts are the draw-downs.

> *How poor did he make his clients on the way to making them rich? That's the big question.*
>
> B. R.

The big question to ask any commodity broker is not, "How much did I make?" It's, "How much did I lose? Don't tell me how rich you've made me. Tell me how broke I went on the way to getting rich. Most importantly, would I have lived through it? Or would I have died of terminal financial cancer?"

Let's take an example. I find a money manager who's made 50 percent a year on his accounts for 10 years. Now, that's enticing. I want to consider trading with him, until I look more closely at his record. When I look at his record, I see that three out of four times, if I gave him $10,000 to invest, before it got to be $20,000, it would have dropped to $5,000. In other words, on the way to doubling my money, three out of four times he first lost half of it.

If that's the case, I'm out of there. Wouldn't you be? Let's put it in larger terms to see the impact. Let's say it's $100,000. You give a money manager $100,000 with the anticipation he's going to increase it. It's your hard-earned money, it's real dollars to you, not something filling a satchel you found on a park bench.

Now, before making you money, you find out he's lost half of it. You're down to $50,000. If you're like me, you're nervous. I start worrying if it gets down to 80 percent. If it's drawn down to 60 percent, I've quit. God forbid I should still be there by the time it gets to 50 percent. I'd be shooting my broker and the money manager. Wouldn't you?

So what you look for in a disclosure document is the *worst performance*.

WORST PERFORMANCE

The only sane way to look at investing (whether it is commodities, stocks, bonds, real estate—I don't care what) is to assume that luck is always an element of investing. And for you, the luck is all bad.

Of course, you may have good luck. But, you can't count on it. The only thing you can count on is bad luck.

So, when you look at a disclosure statement from a money manager, what you look for is this. You find out how much money you would have lost if you started your account on the worst day of the worst week of the worst month of the worst year this money manager ever had.

Then, just ask yourself these three simple questions:

1. "Would I have had to add money to the account that was started on the worst day of the worst month, etc . . . ?"

If the answer is yes, then move on. You're not investing in commodities to lose so much of your capital that you have to invest more. If the money manager loses that much, you don't need him. You're perfectly capable of losing money on your own! You need him to make money.

2. "Would I ever have gotten a margin call?"

A margin call means that the money manager invested so much of your money that he didn't hold enough back in reserve to handle any margin calls. In other words, if you put up $100,000, to talk in even figures, he should have gone into the market with 10 or 20 percent. But, if he went in with 50 percent or 70 percent and trades turned against him, you could get a margin call.

You don't want margin calls. You're not hiring a money manager so that you get margin calls. Forget him.

3. "Would I be uncomfortable with the greatest draw-down that this money manager has ever had?"

Can you stand to lose 5 percent of your money on the way to making a fortune? What about 10 percent? Or 20 percent? Or 30, 40, or 50 percent? What's your pain threshold? How much financial pain can you stand before you have to race in there and rip the remaining money out of the money manager's hand?

If it's 30 percent, has this money manager ever drawn his accounts down below 30 percent? If he has, find a different manager. He's not for you.

Note: This is certainly not a surefire method. You could hire a money manager who in 10 years never had a draw-down greater than 30 percent and in the year you hire him, his draw-down is 50 percent. That happened to me! (I told you, I've made all the mistakes.) Of course, this money manager bounced right back and then doubled his accounts. But how many were left? How many people can stand losing half their money on the way to doubling it.

WHAT COMES AFTER WINNING— SETTING UP PARAMETERS

Thus far we've looked at the down side, at losing. But what if your money manager wins? Then what? The answer is simple, then he loses. You have to assume that after your money manager doubles your money, he's going to draw it down.

So you have to set up some parameters or guidelines that he can follow. Remember, your goal is not to sit around looking over his shoulder. That can drive you as nuts as investing the money yourself.

If you can't pay attention to the trades, then you have to pay attention to your equity.

B. R.

Setting Stop-Losses

In commodity trading a "stop-loss" is an order that is executed only if the price rises or falls beyond a certain point. For example, you're trading British pounds and the pound is at $1.75 U.S. You're going long assuming the pound will increase in value relative to the dollar. But, you can't be positive, so you issue a stop-loss order that essentially says, "If the price goes against me and drops to $1.70, close out my position. At that price I'll assume I guessed wrong and I'll take my loss and leave."

I think stop-loss commodity orders are foolish. They are absentee trader orders. What you're really doing is telling the broker that you won't or can't be there to watch the trade. So, in the event it goes against you, here's what to do. It's like an instruction.

But in commodities, you should be there to watch the trade . . . or your money manager and broker should be there. If it begins going against you and if the system being used says that it was wrong and the trend isn't there, you should get out *immediately*—not wait until the price, in this case, drops an arbitrary five cents. On the other hand, if the system says the trend is there, this is only a little seesaw in the price, you may stay in there, even after it drops seven cents, because you know it's on the way to $2.00.

Stop-loss commodity orders are sucker plays for those who really don't belong in the market—but not stop-loss *equity* orders.

Here are the parameters that you give to your money manager regarding your money.

Let's say that I hire the XYZ brokerage firm to manage my money. The first thing you have to understand is that they are going to manage, not me. Consequently, I give them a limited power of attorney.

Limited Power of Attorney

The purpose here is to allow the money manager to do his thing. The power of attorney allows the money manager to trade in commodities on your account, but without having to ask you each time there's a trade.

It's important to understand that the limited power of attorney *applies only to trading.* The money in my account remains mine; it is insured and thereby protected from fraud. The only way I lose is if the money manager makes bad trades.

Now, I've given him the power to trade, what I need to do is to set the parameters of that trading. This amounts to setting a stop-loss order on the up side and another stop-loss order on the down side. On the next page is my letter of instructions.

Basically what the order I've given says is this (we'll assume a $100,000 account for ease of description):

1. *Rule #1*—If my account drops from $100,000 to $60,000 in value, close out the account. Don't bother to call me—just do it. The idea here is that I am willing to accept a draw-down of 40 percent or $40,000. For practical purposes if the money manager draws the account down by 35 to 40 percent, you made a mistake in hiring him.
2. *Rule #2*—If my account goes from $100,000 to $140,000, liquidate the account and send me the $40,000. The idea on the top side here is to make sure that the money manager doesn't start handling

---

LETTER OF INSTRUCTIONS

Dear Sirs,

I have opened a commodity account with _____
and have given you the trading authority. This letter
is to set the parameters under which I give you that
trading authority.

(1) Should my equity, as of the close of any
     business day decline from original
     deposit to 60% of the original deposit
     (adjusted for additions or withdrawals),
     you are not to institute any new trades
     and are to liquidate all existing trades
     at market as soon as practical at the
     end of any month.

(2) Should my equity increase from the
     original deposit to 140% of original
     deposit (adjusted for additions or with-
     drawals), and remain there at the end of
     any month, you are to send me the 40%
     profits and to then reinstitute the cut-
     off point of #1.

(3) Quarterly, I shall review performance
     and determine how much of the profits I
     will remove.

Any changes in the above instructions should be
obtained from the undersigned.

Sincerely,

Date: _____

A letter of instructions to your broker.

this as a bigger account. It's a $100,000 account (in this case) and it's intended to stay that way. The profits are not plowed back into the account. (Given the leverage of commodities, there's no reason they should be.)

3. *Rule #3*—Start over with Rule #1.

INSTRUCTIONS TO BROKER

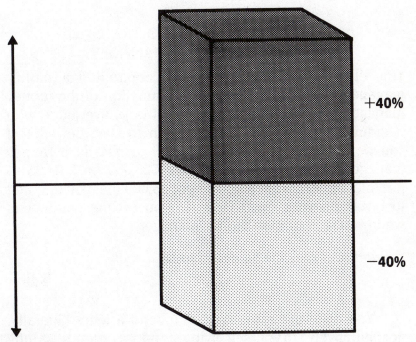

+40%

−40%

An illustration of instructions to your broker.

Consider what this approach does. First, it allows you to follow your equity very easily and quickly. You may not be able to follow the trades your money manager is making. But you darn well can follow how your money is doing. And if it goes bad, you're out. On the other hand, if your manager does well, you've got the profits, not him.

Second, this approach limits your risk from the money manager. Assuming that he doesn't draw down the account right off the bat, you're taking money out. If you ever do get hit, you've already taken out more money than you've put in. So you leave at a profit.

DOING IT WHEN YOU'RE
YOUR OWN MONEY MANAGER

This chapter is about hiring and controlling a money manager. But, as I've said, the real function of the money manager is to be that judiciary, that objective judge who decides when to pull out and when to stay. But what if you don't have $100,000 or $50,000 to give to a money manager? What if you don't have $25,000 or $10,000 to put into a pool? What if you've got $5,000 that you're going to invest on your own? How do you set the parameters when you're your own money manager?

Self-discipline is the hardest discipline of all.

B. R.

You do it the same way. You send a letter (literally, not figuratively) to yourself giving stop-loss orders on equity for the up side and the down side. If you lose $5,000, you'll pull out and find some other way to handle your commodity investing. If you make $2,000 on your $5,000, you put it away and continue to play with the original $5,000. (With only $5,000 to spend, I figure you have to lose it all before quitting . . . after all, that could be only one or two trades.)

Of course, there are differences. The biggest is what you do with your profits. As I've frequently said, if you're making big money in commodities (taking $40,000 in profits out each time), my suggestion is that you stick it into short-term real estate. On the other hand, if your profits are more modest, $2,000 each time as in our example, then my suggestion is that you bank it. If you're doing well at all, very soon you'll have enough ($50,000 or more) so that you can afford a real money manager.

FIRING A MONEY MANAGER

The easiest thing in the world to do is to hire someone. The hardest is to fire him.

Even when your reasons are obvious, valid, and strong, firing is still difficult. Your money manager has lost 40 percent. You're going to pull your account and go elsewhere. Except that he's a nice guy and he's had a string of bad luck that'll probably never happen again and he needs the business and now he's really hungry.

So you leave the remaining $60,000 (or $30,000 or whatever) with him.

Bad move, right? Of course it's bad. But how hard-hearted can you be? It's one thing to sit here reading this book saying to yourself, "Yes, if the money manager draws down the account 35 to 40 percent, I'll get out." It's quite another to talk to him eyeball-to-eyeball or even over the phone and do it. Let me give you an example.

As an asset manager, I hire and fire money managers all the time. That's what I'm paid to do, watch the money managers for my clients.

One time I hired this money manager who we'll call Fred (obviously not his real name). Fred had all the right stuff. He had a great track record, had never drawn his accounts down more than 20 percent, had a good system, and stuck to it with great discipline. He was undoubtedly a winner.

He was also a winner in his personal life. He had married in his later 30s, but always wanted children. Now in his 40s, he was blessed with a child, a lovely daughter. He was the happiest man in the world.

ASSET MANAGER

Broker	**Broker**	**Broker**
Commodities	Stocks–Bonds	Real Estate

Investment Investment Investment Investment Investment Investment

An asset manager selects money managers or brokers for you. The asset manager also keeps watch over all your investments in every area—he is the ultimate judiciary.

The only concern I had with Fred was that at times I thought he might have a gambled a bit with the accounts—not enough to hurt anybody, but more than I was comfortable with. But now that he's a family man, he's no longer gambling. He doesn't want to leave home anymore; he doesn't want to take any unnecessary risks. He's just ready to work with discipline.

Not only is Fred professionally excellent, but now his personal life has gotten excellent. At this point I thought about having an "exclusive" with Fred. (I and my accounts would be his only client.) He was the perfect commodities money manager.

Then, one day, Fred discovers that his lovely daughter has leukemia. It's one of those rapidly developing forms, and the child is forced into the hospital almost immediately.

For seven months Fred is in the hospital with the child. He runs his business from the hospital by phone.

Now, if you didn't know about Fred's personal life and just read his track record, you'd be happy to put your money with him. But I already had put my accounts with him, and I knew about what was happening to him personally.

> *To thine own self be true.*
>
> William Shakespeare, *Hamlet*

I had a terribly difficult decision to make. On the one hand, Fred was a good person who had fallen upon terrible times. My heart said that I should support him in his time of need.

On the other hand, my head wondered how much attention Fred would be able to pay to his accounts, given the fact that he was always in the hospital with his daughter. Would he still be the top flight money manager he had always been? Or would he become something else?

I'm paid to worry about other people's money. I have a fiduciary responsibility to clients who are counting on me to manage their assets. That means I have to put their money ahead of my heart. (If I don't, I don't belong doing what I do.)

So I pulled all my accounts away from Fred. That represented, at the time, more than half of his business.

He and I, besides being business associates, were also friends. He came to me in my office and said something like, "How could you do this? You know that right now is when I need those accounts the most. You know my track record . . . I've never let you down. How could you be so callous?"

It broke my heart—he was right on all counts! But I had my job to do. From that time on, Fred and I were no longer friends. And he no longer wants to handle my accounts.

As it turned out, the money he had under management dropped by attrition of accounts and by losses by a factor of close to 90 percent. A lot of that was my withdrawing accounts. But a lot of it was also that he began to lose money, lots of money.

When I left, it was at a profit. Others who weren't privy to what was happening to him, the pressure he was under, weren't so fortunate.

There's another moral to this story. Eventually Fred's daughter died. He recovered from this blow and had another child. He went back to his business and built it up again.

At that point I would have liked to have him back, but he didn't want to come back.

I knew when I fired him that I ran that risk, that I might alienate him permanently. That was one of the chances that I took.

The worst habit is hope.

B. R.

So don't tell me it's easy to fire a money manager. Don't tell me that you don't have the heart to do it, that maybe the losses were just a fluke and if you stayed with him things would work out. Don't tell me you can't face him or even call him on the phone to talk to him about dropping him because he'll be so upset. Don't tell me any of it because I've been through worse than you.

Yet, I did it. And if I had it to do over again, I'd make the same decision. When it's time to fire a money manager, you have to do it, no matter how difficult it may be.

For those who are their own money managers, the same applies. Let's face it. You may be lousy at investing your own money. Or you may have your own emotional problems that are putting enormous pressure on you. Or other factors may apply.

When you've drawn your own account down to whatever stop-loss you've entered for yourself, *fire yourself.* You just aren't fit to handle your money.

One of the advantages of doing it yourself is that you can always rehire yourself. Maybe you take six months off of investing to learn the fundamentals of the commodities you're interested in. Or maybe it takes a while for you to straighten out your personal life so that you aren't under emotional pressure and can think straight again.

When that happens, you can always rehire yourself. Maybe the second time (or the third or the fourth), it'll turn out that you're a great money manager.

THE MONEY MANAGER WHO'S RIGHT FOR YOU

Yes, the perfect money manager for you does exist. It may be you, yourself, if you have a small amount to start with. Or it may be a high-powered money manager who's handling millions and will only accept an account of $100,000.

It doesn't matter. One way or another, you need a money manager. Just be careful when you pick one.

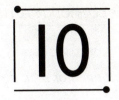

10

GETTING STARTED— NO MATTER HOW MUCH MONEY YOU HAVE

The best way to get started is to start rich.

B. R.

Take your $100,000 or $50,000 and find yourself a good money manager, as detailed in earlier chapters. If you choose right, he'll make you richer than Midas in a few years.

Of course, we don't all start rich. I know I sure didn't, and I expect that many of you are in that same situation. So you're starting off something less than rich. Instead of $50,000, you've got $5,000 or maybe only $2,500. How do you get started?

*For all sad words of tongue or pen, the saddest are these,
"It might have been."*

John Greenleaf Whittier, "Maud Muller"

YOUR ALTERNATIVES WITH AROUND $2,500

There aren't a whole lot of alternatives, but there are a few. If you're lucky you can find a pool to invest your money in. A broker's recommendation is your best bet here. (Pools were discussed at length in an earlier chapter.)

On the other hand, if you can't find a pool, you can always invest yourself. You can open your own commodities account and start trading. Only if you've only got around $2,500, you better be lucky as well as smart because you've got to hit it right the first time out . . . otherwise, you'll have lost your capital and you'll have to wait till you earn another $2,500 before you can try again. (That doesn't mean you should stop trying. All you need to do is to connect once and you could be on your way.)

My personal feeling is that you really need about $5,000 as a minimum to get started. You may only need $2,500 or even $1,500 to open a contract. But unless your timing is perfect, you can be right and still lose, initially. With $5,000 to back it up, you can avoid some of the bumps along the way.

MINIMUM NET WORTH REQUIREMENTS TO OPEN AN ACCOUNT

One problem that I hear people who don't have a lot of money complain about is that "minimum net worth requirements" that brokerage houses require in order to trade. You go to Shearson or Smith-Barney or Merrill Lynch and they tell you that in addition to the cash you will put up for the trade (your $2,500 or whatever), you're also going to need $50,000 or $100,000 in net worth, exclusive of your house, before they'll accept your account. What are they talking about and why?

Net worth is net worth. It's all the cash, stocks, bonds, real estate, furniture, the dog and cat . . . whatever you own that isn't being used as collateral for loans. If you have to have $50,000 or more, what it sounds like the brokerage house is saying is that they only want the fat cats to trade. They only want those people who have accumulated wealth to get in on the commodities gravy train.

Not so. It's simply a matter of "suitability." When you open an account with a brokerage house, you create a "fiduciary" relationship with that house. They have a duty to protect your interests. One of the ways the law says that that duty is expressed is to determine whether or not you are suitable to trade.

> *You can fool all of the people some of the time, and you*
> *can fool some of the people all of the time, but you cannot*
> *fool all of the people all of the time.*
> Attributed to Abraham Lincoln and Phineas Barnum

There are lots of tests for this. One is that you understand what commodities trading is all about as evidenced by the fact that you've traded commodities before, or that you've bought and sold stocks or bonds or CDs or that you had a checking or savings account or a piggy bank when you were a kid. In other words, you're savvy in the world of investing.

(If you think the brokerage house cares a whit whether you're savvy or not, you're really naive . . . read on.)

Another test of suitability is whether you can afford to lose the money you invest. Let's face it, as we've seen in the chapters of this book, a commodity trade can go against you, and you could lose your entire investment in a very short time. Can you survive such a loss? Supposedly if you have a net worth of $50,000 or more (or whatever the current minimum is in your brokerage house), you can.

(Once again, if you think the brokerage house cares in the least whether or not you can afford to lose the money, I know someone with a New York bridge who would love to sell it to you.)

And there are one or two other tests of minor consequence. Okay. So the brokerage house doesn't care if you are suitable or not. Why do they go through so much trouble to be sure that you at least qualify according to their tests?

The reason is simple. They don't want to be sued. If you take your mother's last $3,000 of retirement money, open an account and make an unsuccessful trade . . . chances are you are going to get a lawyer who will claim that you didn't know what you were getting into, you were suckered into it by the broker, and you couldn't afford to lose the money. The lawyer will argue that you were "unsuitable" to be trading commodities. And, according to the law in most states and the regulations that brokers work under, that lawyer will win, and the brokerage house will have to make good your losses as well as possible damages. Now, no brokerage house is going to be thrilled to do that.

Consequently, they all have this form. It asks for your net worth, your experience, and other factors influencing your suitability. You fill it out and sign it, swearing that it's the truth, and you're in business.

Do the brokerage houses check out the form you signed to see if it's truth? No. Why should they? They don't care if you can afford to lose the money or not. They don't care if it's grandma's last shekel. All that they care about is that you *filled out and signed the form*. Once you do that, you can't sue them. You can't come back and say you didn't know or weren't suitable because you signed in ink that you were.

So, you see, anyone can open a commodities account at any time regardless of their financial condition—if they're willing to jump through the hoops that the brokerage houses set up. Just remember: It's your money and your business what you do with it.

Once you give the brokerage house an indication, in writing, that you can afford the loss, you're trading. They're dying to let you trade.

LARGE MINIMUM MARGIN ACCOUNTS

Another problem that investors who start off small sometimes run into is the minimum amount required to trade. Say you want to trade a contract of sugar. The margin requirement of the commodities exchange is $1,000. But your broker won't let you trade until you put up $5,000. You're told that's the minimum account size needed to trade a single contract of sugar.

Of course it's baloney. There's no law saying that. It's not necessary. (Although from a practical standpoint, you want to put up more money than the minimum margin in case the price goes momentarily against you.)

Always act within your own level of comfort, not the other guy's level of comfort.

B. R.

The brokerage house just wants to feel comfortable. In case the trade goes against you, they've got your extra money to back it up. Also, once you've deposited the money in their account, they have a better chance of getting you to spring for the next trade.

To insure this, the brokerage house may require a large account. (This is in addition to your margin account and maintenance account explained earlier.) A "brokerage account" is an account from which money can be tapped to fill up your margin and maintenance accounts. Let's say that the margin is $1,000 and the maintenance is also $1,000. You need $2,000 to open the trade. If the trade goes against you, your margin is whittled down. The brokerage house automatically takes money from your maintenance account and dumps it into your margin account. Remember, the house must maintain minimum margins at all times. (That guarantees that the losers are able to pay the winners.)

However, the house says it still wants $5,000. (I've seen brokerage houses set up in such a way that in order to trade you have to put $7,000 for a $1,000 minimum!) In this case if a trade goes against you, the house dumps money from the $2,500 brokerage account into the maintenance account and from that into the margin account—$5,000 to trade a $1,000 contract.

If you don't have the $5,000, go elsewhere. There are almost as many brokers as there are gnats on a horse's tail. Find another one who is more reasonable about the minimums and who will take $2,000 or $2,500 to trade a $1,000 minimum contract. (You can try arguing with a broker who requires a large account, but you may be wasting your breath. If it's a big company, chances are it's the firm's policy and our individual broker may have nothing to say about it.)

GETTING YOUR PROFITS OUT

Let's say that you start an account with $2,000. You read that the Secretary of the Treasury is going to drive the dollar down in value (which, as noted earlier, is a real announcement that a Treasury Secretary in former President Reagan's Cabinet made). He says he's going to drive the dollar down, and you're smart enough to realize that this is a buy signal for foreign currencies if ever there was one.

You're smart enough to know where to invest, so you go long on the deutsche marks—one contract. As luck would have it, the very next day deutsche marks go up. At the end of the second day, your $2,000 account is worth $4,000.

What do you do now?

You have two options. You can call up your broker and tell him to issue your a check for the $2,000 profit. He'll do it. You can take your profits out every day in cash.

They should shoot the man who said, "It never hurts to take a profit."

B. R.

———

Or you can let it sit there. If you let it sit there, you are creating a reserve in case the market turns against you.

Let's say that within a few weeks your $2,000 investment is up to $5,000, all of which you let sit in your account. Now the market turns against you. There's a lot of sentiment that says that the dollar has fallen too far too fast, the deutsche marks have risen too high too quickly.

Now it's tough. It was easy to see sit there and feel satisfied when your account has gone from $2,000 to $5,000. It's quite a bit different when it's gone from $5,000 back to $2,000. As noted in an earlier chapter, now's when the judiciary comes in to decide whether you're temporarily going broke on the way to getting rich, or whether you're going broke period.

The point here, however, is that by leaving your profits in the account you have the option of making that decision. The $3,000 in profit was there for you to lose. If you had taken your profits out earlier, it would be gone and the brokerage house would have traded you out.

But, you say, that makes no sense. Maybe not in a managed account, but if you're trading one contract for yourself, you've got to go for broke. You've got to make it on the major moves. You've got to pray that your account goes back up to $10,000 or $25,000, when you can trade out. Leaving your early profits in there allows you that freedom.

I can't think of the number of times I've seen prices shoot up, then come all the way back down before taking off for the skies. You don't want to miss that comet ride.

IRAs, KEOGHs, AND OTHER RETIREMENT PLANS

Most people say that IRAs, KEOGHs and other retirement plans are strictly for super-safe money. That's the *last* money you'd want to invest in a high risk area such as commodities. Even the government generally prohibits your using such funds for individual commodities trades.

I say that's baloney. Those other people are strictly looking at the downside risk. But what about the up side? Remember, in most retirement accounts *there's no tax to pay immediately in the year you receive gain*. All profits are deferred until you're 55 or whenever you begin drawing down the account. (By then, hopefully, you're in a lower tax bracket.) If your goal is to make a profit, the pension plans are the ideal investment medium. None of the profits are immediately taxable. What could be better?!

Of course, there is that government regulation that says you can't invest your pension money in a commodities account. (Is the government just trying to protect you? Or is it making sure it can tax those wonderful commodities gains?)

There is a way, however—a commodities mutual fund or managed account. Such accounts are set up in such a way that they have a maximum draw-down, say 35 percent of the account's value. If the account is drawn down, you're out. Because of this, you can't lose more than you put up, which is the big argument used against trading commodities in pension accounts. (Remember, in managed commodities accounts, you never trade all your capital. At the most you'll have one-third out there in contracts. The rest is always held in reserve.)

Also, with a managed account you're not doing the trading or having a broker do the trading. You're not in there picking and choosing what to buy and when to sell. It's all handled as part of a managed portfolio.

So, if you have enough money to afford a money manager or a mutual fund (we're not talking big bucks here—perhaps $10,000), why not use your pension fund for commodities trading?

If it still bothers you, just remember, don't only look on the down side. Look on the up side . . . look at all those untaxed profits!

TOP TRADES
FOR THE '90s

Now that you know how to handle yourself with commodity futures, or at least know where the landmines are, you should be ready to make your move toward future profits. Only where are those moves going to be?

It would take a pretty good crystal ball to foresee the top trades of the next few years, and while, like most people, my hindsight is 100 percent, my foresight remains somewhat clouded. Certainly neither I nor anyone else can predict with any degree of certainty what will or will not happen in the commodity market.

Nevertheless, I am going to make a stab in the dark. From my perspective of the very end of the 1980s, I'm going to give you commodities picks which I think will perform well in the coming years. If I'm right, you can send plaudits to me care of my newsletter, *Roszel's Survival Strategies*, 33 S. Allison Parkway, Suite 302, Lakewood, CO 80226. If I'm wrong, pretend you saw the following picks in someone else's book or newsletter.

Note: The following recommendations are *long term* trends. In the short run, the positions may be reversed, increased, or decreased. Prudent money management may call for *no* position during times of congestion.

CRUDE OIL—LONG

I believe oil is headed higher over the early 1990s. There are a multitude of reasons for this not the least of which is the end of the Iran–Iraq war. While that war was on, neither country adhered to production restraints; both sought to sell as much oil as possible to further their war efforts.

With the war ended, OPEC (Organization of Petroleum Exporting Countries) appears to be reestablishing control over production in the Middle East. (Both Iran and Iraq are OPEC members.) Saudi Arabia has curtailed its production as have other member countries. This caused a significant increase in oil prices by the middle of 1989. Continued production curtailment could result in higher prices into the 1990s.

GOLD—LONG/SILVER—LONG

Both gold and silver have been down in the dumps for several years. Although they have made attempts at price increases, these have repeatedly been beaten back by a bear market. As of this writing, they seem to be sinking to lower levels.

The major reason for the problems with precious metals is that they are in overproduction. Gold can profitably be produced for prices in excess of $300 per ounce. Silver can profitably be produced for prices in excess of $4 an ounce. Since prices have continuously been above this level for most of the last decade, producers have been encouraged to increase levels of production. The result has been a sluggish, bearish market.

Inflation, however, is on the rise as of this writing, and precious metals are inflation-sensitive. If inflation begins to take off (read the early chapters of this book), investors will begin to look for hedges, and gold and silver are tops on that list. At some point the demand caused by inflation is going to catch up with the oversupply caused by overproduction, and at that point the price should zoom.

Beware, however, of false starts and falling prices until then. The bottom is difficult to predict, but it certainly is under $6 and probably close to $4 for silver and under $400 and probably close to $300 for gold.

GRAINS (WHEAT, SOYBEANS, CORN, ETC.)— LONG/SHORT

The reason for the double recommendation here has to do with changes in global weather patterns. I don't care whether you call it the "Greenhouse effect" or "ozone depletion" or something else, one thing seems certain— the weather is changing.

The result is that areas of the world which previously had been wet are getting drier and some areas which had been dry are getting wetter. Thus we are seeing drought in the Midwest, the breadbowl of the United States.

In 1988 the Midwest drought coincided with droughts in other grain-growing regions of the world. As a result the total world supply of grains was drawn down from

100 days (where it had been for decades) to under 50 days—all in one year! While as of this writing, 1989 appears to be a far better year with more moisture in critical areas and more farmers planting in other areas, it's still going to be tight.

The result is that into the 1990s we are likely to see occasional periods of drought as well as periods of more normal weather. Grains can be expected to respond with dramatically higher prices in some years followed by near normal or even lower prices in other years.

To win at grains you always had to watch the weather. But at least in the past, the weather wasn't always so extreme. Now we are faced with extremes in weather that could result in extremes in grain prices.

Obviously I can't say which years to go long and which years to go short. But check the weather reports for the Midwest in December and in the spring. Droughts don't happen all at once—they come upon us over a period of months.

Also, be aware that after a drought year when grain prices are high, farmers worldwide tend to plant more grain crops to cash in on the higher prices. As a result, *unless the drought in the second year is as severe or more so than in the first*, grain prices historically tend to fall in the year after a drought ends.

COFFEE AND ORANGE JUICE—AVOID

I never trade anything I can drink. The reason is simply that in my opinion there's too much manipulation of these markets.

FINANCIAL INSTRUMENTS—LONG/SHORT

Financial instruments such as T-Bills, notes, GNMA Certs., etc. are all interest-rate sensitive. Over the 1990s I flatly predict we are going to have great volatility in our interest rates.

You'll just have to watch the rates closely and decide whether it's the correct time to go high or to go low.

CURRENCIES—DEUTSCHE MARK—SHORT, THEN LONG/YEN—SHORT

If there's any "monkey business" in the market, the worst of it traditionally has been in the money pits, probably worst of all, the Japanese yen. Recent efforts by government overseers, however, have straightened out many of these problems.

Even so, during the last half of the 1980s, the big money was to be found in currencies, specifically the Japanese yen. It isn't often that a Secretary of the Treasury and a Chairman of the Federal Reserve come right out and say they are going to drive their currency down. But that's what happened in 1985, and the dollar plunged while the yen and other foreign currencies soared during the same period.

Since then, the U.S. government has attempted to keep our currency at around 120–140 yen to the dollar. Such efforts, however, failed in the early part of 1989 and possibly later for a single reason—higher interest rates. To counter the threat of inflation, the Fed raised interest rates and this did result in a firmer dollar.

As the United States eases over into a recession after 1990, however, interest rates may again fall (at least temporarily) and when they do, the dollar may likewise plummet once more as foreigners exhibit their general distaste for our currency.

Watch domestic interest rates and our trade debt. If the trade debt doesn't fall *significantly* and interest rates do, that'll be the sign that it could be the right time to go long in foreign currency.

The currency of preference is the deutsche mark. Many investors see Germany as a stable economy which will benefit from problems in the United States.

At the same time, investors see problems with the yen. This is based both in technical and fundamental signals. Technically, all of '79 to '85 saw the yen as stable and flat in relation to the dollar. Then in '85 we saw a sudden rise in the yen which continued until the beginning of 1988.

By contrast, all of '88 was fairly constant for the yen when compared to normal volatility over the past 10 years. Thus we appear to have seen a setting point which is typically followed by a reversal in prices and market direction.

Fundamentally, the problem for the yen is that the Japanese cannot flex their financial muscles as well as they could two years ago. While debt in the United States is heavy, Japan is expected to incur more future debt with spending on its own defense. In addition, U.S. companies have learned to better compete or integrate with Japanese firms.

MY THOUGHTS

These, then, are some of my thoughts regarding futures at the time this book is written. Of course, by the time you read this we could be in hyperinflation or in a world war or, praise the Lord, in peace and economic harmony.

All of which is to say that you should take these recommendations with a grain of salt. But there's one recommendation you should take at face value—my first recommendation that if you want to be amongst the "haves" in the 1990s, you need to be investing in commodities as soon as possible.

APPENDIX I
HOW TO TRADE
COMMODITIES

It's often been said that the greatest asset of a commodities trader is a strong bladder. The implication is that things happen fast and furious and you can't take time out, even for personal necessities.

While that certainly may be true for floor traders (those who actually handle the orders on the floors of the exchanges) and even in some situations for brokers, it certainly isn't true for you. Your goal should be to trade for trends. That is, you're looking to latch onto big price swings, either up or down, and ride them for big profits.

DAY TRADING

Trading for trends virtually eliminates the pressure of "day trading" where you trade into and out of a commodity sometimes in more than one trade within a single day hoping for short bursts of profits. There are speculators who do this, sitting in a commodities broker's office, watching the price movements and trying to take advantage of them.

However, unless you're actually a broker on the floor of an exchange, it's been shown that in most cases day traders lose money. There are many reasons for this, two of which are facts noted earlier in this book. First, even the best computer systems are wrong 60 percent of the time, and to profit you need to catch onto those 40 percent trends and ride them for all they're worth. Day traders are in and out too fast to do this.

The second reason is that there is occasional market manipulation (as revealed in recent government "sting" operations) by floor traders who execute your orders. If you're catching a trend, it won't matter if you lose a tick or two (a "tick" is the smallest price movement which floor traders can shave off of your order). To a day trader, however, it can mean the difference between profit or loss.

GOING LONG IN SILVER

Thus, what you're going to do, I hope, is speculate in the futures market looking to ride a long-term trend. You're going to place your order and—unless the market immediately turns against you—let it stay in there. The easiest way to see how this is done is to take two examples. In the first, you'll be going long, buying a commodity. In the second, involving soybeans, you'll be going short, selling a commodity.

It is January of 1979 and you've heard rumblings about the silver market. The spot (current) price of silver stands at $4.80. This represents a fairly high price for silver, considering that it has been as low as $2.00 an ounce only a few years earlier. However, recently it had risen toward the $5.00 range, only to fall back.

Many savvy investors are going short (selling silver) on the theory that it's reached a high and will rapidly fall back to previous lows under $4.00. There are reports that major purchasers of silver, such as the photograph industry and private coin minters, are holding off purchasing silver, waiting for lower prices.

You've been studying fundamentals and reading investors' newsletters which have suggested, however, that for the first time in decades, there is a potential silver shortage. The economy is going very strong, and industrial demand for silver is on the upswing. At the same time, plagued by years of low prices, silver production is way behind. New mines have not been built, and old mines are offering poor yields. As a result, demand exceeds supply and there is very little excess supply left to make up the difference.

On top of this, the country, in the midst of the Carter Administration, is plagued by inflation which is now entering double digits. Pundits on television are forecasting that within a few years inflation will soar to triple digits. Never mind that this is a worst case scenario. The public is scared and for the first time since the 1920s, investors are looking seriously at inflation hedges.

Silver, like its cousin gold, is an inflation hedge. Silver is known to be resistant to inflationary pressures. That is, as the value of the dollar goes down, the price of silver tends to go up.

You are beginning to believe that silver is poised to make a major market move upward, one that you might be able to take advantage of. However, you wait to see what the technical signals indicate.

From a price of $4.80, within just two weeks, silver moves up to $5.20. The new highs exceed the prices of the previous month's trading, which is a strong bullish technical signal. Many speculators who had gone short (sold) silver are having to cover their contracts. Though the bearish sentiment in the market remains strong (that silver will soon fall in value), you're beginning to think that the opposite might be true.

At about this time, news stories begin to break on the regular evening and morning news shows about how inflation is causing ever more concern to people and how they are seeking hedges. Silver is mentioned as one of those hedges.

At about the same time, a national news magazine read by investors does an article on the probability that silver might move significantly higher.

You are almost convinced, but continue to wait. Then the National Silver Institute releases figures showing that photographic usage of silver is reaching an all-time high. Photography, as you recall, is the single greatest user of silver.

At the same time, you read in a national financial journal that jewelry sales are increasing during the current boom period as people in general seek to find inflation hedges and opt for jewelry.

You make a decision. It looks to you as though silver is going to make a major move upward. Of course, you can't be sure. But you're willing to risk a contract on it.

You open a single contract for 5,000 ounces of September silver at $5.60 an ounce. What this means is that you put up a margin of $1,500 which guarantees that come September (remember, it's currently February) you will buy 5,000 ounces at $5.60 an ounce. (The difference between the future price of $5.60 in September and the current "spot" price of $5.20 is the carrying charge for silver during that period.)

Of course, you have no intention of really buying any physical silver. Hopefully, before September the price will go up and you'll be able to execute an offsetting contract receiving a substantial profit. That's your up side.

Your down side is that you could be totally wrong and the "experts" could be right. Silver might be at a peak and ready to plunge downward. To counter against this you are ready to issue an offsetting trade the moment silver shows severe weakness. You could put in a stop-loss order that would trade you out of silver at, for example, $5.40, a twenty cent or $1,000 loss. But you prefer to watch the market closely and issue the order yourself when it falls. You don't want to be closed out of your position on a dip just before the market resumes a straight upward course.

Fortunately for you, the price of silver moves steadily upward. Within two weeks, the September contract is at $5.90. You've made yourself a profit, should you take it, of $1,500. You review.

All the fundamentals suggest the shortage in silver is continuing. In addition, silver is regularly breaking into new all-time highs, an excellent technical signal. You decide to sit tight.

A week later an investors' newsletter announces that a very large photographic company has decided to stop waiting for silver prices to fall. Instead, it is buying. At the same time a major minter of private silver coins announces that it has fired its silver buyer and is instituting a new plan of regular purchases.

Silver prices almost explode on the news. Coupled with actual physical shortages, speculators are pouring into the market going long. A big grin begins to form on your face. This is going to not only be one of the few major moves of the year, it could be one of the biggest moves of the decade.

Silver continues upward and as your month of September approaches, it has reached the incredible price of $20.25 an ounce! You have made a profit of nearly $75,000 on your initial $1,500 investment.

Again you reevaluate. Your contract will expire soon. You have several options:

1. You can purchase the physical silver for $5.60 an ounce.
2. You can trade out of your contract and realize your profit.
3. You can "roll over" your contract into a later month. (You trade out of your current contract and open a new one—there may be a slight loss during the roll-over [depending on the month you select], but in general you're simply keeping your trade open.)

You look around and realize that silver is the talk on everyone's lips. It's even getting major stories in the national news magazines. For the first time in history, the evening news shows are showing the price of silver right along with the Dow Jones Averages.

You also read that physical silver is pouring into the country. India, which reportedly has 300 million ounces available, is sending shiploads, even though the export of silver from the country is supposedly illegal. In addition silver mines in Mexico and elsewhere are working around the clock to increase production. Finally, on TV you see huge lines of people turning in their silverware, old coins, anything containing silver to local coin dealers and pawn shops.

In your mind you begin to wonder what effect all these new supplies of silver will have on the supply/demand ratio. You reason that if these supplies had come on-line before the price shot up, they would certainly have been enough to quench the then-existing demand. Has the demand increased so much more than that?

You look at the technical signals. Silver is continuing to set new all-time highs. Runaway gaps are still appearing in the charts. All technical signals point to continued price increases.

But, you're conservative and worried. You think that as fast as the price went up, it could also go down. Finally, with the market so bullish on silver, you begin to wonder who's left on the sidelines willing to buy?

So you trade out of the contract and liquidate your profits. (Remember, you can take your profits out daily— you don't have to wait until you trade out.)

Instead of falling in price, silver continues to rise until it reaches $25 an ounce. Then, in a matter of weeks, it doubles again in price reaching an incredible $50 an ounce! Day after day there are limit moves which lock in traders in the back months. Everybody wants to buy silver; nobody can get in.

Silver hovers there for weeks. During the time there are rumbles of problems in the silver pits. Alleged market manipulation by the Hunt Brothers from Texas and others is suggested in the papers. The Chicago Board of Trade, the Commodity Exchange, the MidAmerica Commodity Exchange and the New York Mercantile Exchange, all of whom have silver contracts, announce that they are increasing the margin requirements on silver to reduce speculation. The government announces that investigations into fraud in silver speculation are going to be conducted.

The silver market hangs poised for nearly six weeks as investment pundits cry the silver will now surely go to $100 an ounce. Instead it plunges.

For days at a time there are limit moves downward. Those who are long on silver can't get out. Everyone now wants to *sell* silver! Just as fast as it went up, it goes down bottoming temporarily at between $20 and $25 an ounce. (Eventually, over the next few years, it drops back to under $5 an ounce!)

Now, the question is, did you get out too soon? Or were you lucky to get out while the getting was good? If you can answer that, you're already an experienced trader.

GOING SHORT IN SOYBEANS

It is May 1988 and you are relatively new to trading commodities. Thus far you have only gone long, that is, bought commodities. You aren't exactly sure how to sell short, so you've stayed out of it. Now, however, an opportunity may be arising.

Thus far you've been speculating primarily in the currencies, mainly the Japanese yen, and have done quite well as the U.S. dollar has fallen over a period of more than two years. However, now the dollar seems stabilized at between 120 and 130 yen to the dollar and the opportunity for profit is reduced. You look elsewhere. Grains seem a likely target.

There has been a drought in the grain-growing regions of the United States Nothing too serious thus far, but if it continues, it could mean much higher prices for grains. You begin watching carefully, particularly soybeans which you judge to be especially volatile as determined by previous price movements.

Other speculators are watching as well, and soon the price of soybeans begins to rise. From about $6.50 a bushel when you first begin looking (which represents a four-year high) soybeans move up quickly to $7.00 a bushel.

This is another four-year high and higher than the previous month's high. You begin to think that now might be the time to go long in soybeans.

At about this time, long range weather reports predict far lower than normal precipitation in the Midwest, the prime soybean growing area of the country. This speculation drives the price up to $7.25 a bushel.

In addition, television shows begin featuring pieces about farmers lifting dry soil in their hands and letting it blow away. A respected farm organization reports that the soybean crop could be as much as 35 to 50 percent off of last year's crop.

It is now June and you decide it's time to go long. But even as you try to get into the market the price shoots up to $9.00 a bushel and almost immediately to $9.50. You aren't alone . . . everyone has decided to go long in soybeans.

You pull back. You realize that the time to have bought would have been a month earlier. Now, the trend is already full-blown and well identified. If you buy now, you're buying high. A reversal in the price could wipe you out. So you wait.

During the month of June, the price continues to move upward reaching nearly $11.00 a bushel for soybeans. At the same time, disturbing reports are starting to come in.

Precipitation, mild at first, is occurring in scattered areas of the Midwest. Storms carrying occasional showers pass through. Scenes on television depict soybean farmers saying that it's too little too late. But behind them you see fields flooded with water.

Others have apparently seen this too. For the first time in weeks the price of soybeans does not exceed the previous month's highs. In fact, the price drops nearly 75 cents a bushel. The next day, the long range weather report suggests above normal precipitation for the next 30 days. You decide to short soybeans.

You call your broker and sell one contract of August soybeans for $10.25 a bushel. You put up a margin of $1,500. What this means is that come August, you have to deliver 5,000 bushels of soybeans to someone who guarantees to pay you $10.25 a bushel.

Of course, you don't have any soybeans and have no intention of obtaining any. Your plan is to offset the contract long before it's due, hopefully for a profit. Now you wait.

You don't have to wait long. It's the end of June and rain starts pouring in the Midwest. Suddenly, everyone wants to sell soybeans short and those who were long are scrambling to cover their trades. (They're trying to offset now losing long contracts with short contracts.)

Soybeans plunge within weeks to just above $7.50 a bushel where they momentarily hover. The U.S. Department of Agriculture grain report is due out early in July. It will list the damage done to crops by the now-gone drought. Speculation is rampant that the rain has saved the crops. Only 10 percent of the soybean harvest may have been damaged.

You're thinking about the USDA report. The market has already discounted it by dropping the price of soybeans so dramatically. It would virtually have to say that there was no damage to the crops at all for the price to fall further. On the other hand, if it says that the damage is more than estimated, prices could bounce back up. You decide that it's time to sell.

You make an offsetting trade for $7.75 a bushel. Here's what your trades look like:

Early June	Sold 5,000 bushels at	$10.25
Early July	Bought 5,000 bushels at	7.75
	Profit per bushel	2.50

Note how going short works. You sell *first*, and buy *later*. This is just the opposite, in terms of time, from going long. But the principle is the same. You sell for more than you buy, thus realizing a profit. In this case your profit is $2.50 a bushel and since the contract was for 5,000 bushels, you've made a profit of $12,500. (Not bad on a $1,500 investment, eh!)

A few days later the USDA report comes in. There is a staggering 25 percent crop loss. The price of soybeans shoots back up to over $9.00 a bushel.

By then, however, there have been even more rains and it appears that even this crop loss won't be that significant given existing supplies and the next crop, which will probably be heavier than normal.

You got out at the right time and congratulate yourself on your perspicacity.

SPREADING

These then, are the two basic trades you can make in commodities—going long and going short. There are other more complex trades such as "spreading." This involves buying in one market and simultaneously selling in another. The idea is that you lock in a profit due to disparities for different commodities, months or exchanges. There are basically four types of spreads:

1. The intramarket spread where you go long in one month and short in another month for the same commodity. You hope to profit from disparities in the carrying charges between different months.
2. The intermarket spread where you go long in one commodity exchange and short in another exchange for the *same month* taking advantage of disparities between the months in the two exchanges.
3. The intercommodity spread where you go long in one commodity, for example gold, and short in a closely related commodity, for example silver. You hope to take advantage of the relationship between the two commodities.
4. Product spread where you go long in a basic commodity, for example soybeans, and short in the product of this commodity, for example, soybean oil, hoping to take advantage of manufacturing considerations.

Spreads hinge on a variety of factors such as disparities in the cost of storing a commodity, the cost of insuring it, and the cost of money involved in finance and storage. These generally come under the heading of "carrying charges."

Spreads are sophisticated commodity trades and you should be well versed in the market before attempting them.

THE ROLE OF THE
SPECULATOR IN COMMODITY FUTURES

The commodities markets came into existence in the mid-1800s as devices for the producers of commodities to hedge. "Hedge" means to lock in a price to avoid taking the chance of losing money later on. For example, coffee is selling for $2.00 a pound today, but your crop won't be ready for delivery until three months from now. At today's prices you can make a profit. However, if the price drops between now and when you bring your crop to market, you might sustain a loss.

Consequently, you'd like to hedge. You'd like to sell half of your future crop at today's prices and then sell the other half three months in the future at whatever price is available.

If the price goes up, you'll make a profit on the half you didn't sell today. If it drops, you've still locked in half the crop you sell today at a price which allows a minimal profit for you.

The only thing you need is someone to sell your crop to, three months in advance.

In the mid-1800s, banks took on this task. However, as the demand for "future contracts" increased, a marketplace was created. These were the great commodity exchanges of the Midwest. These came into existence as soon as a new kind of investor was born, the speculator.

The speculator took a position opposite that of the hedger. When the hedger bet that the price would go down, the speculator bet it would go up (going long). When the hedger bet the price would go up, the speculator bet it would go down (going short).

The speculator risked his money in the hopes of generating a profit off the hedger. Note that in order for a futures market to exist, both hedgers and speculators were needed.

Of course, the speculator never intended to actually buy or sell (take physical possession of) a commodity. He intended to trade out with an offsetting contract long before that. The commodity exchange provided him with that opportunity by offering a regulated "floor" where trades could take place in an orderly fashion.

If you enter the commodity market as an investor, your function is that of a *speculator*. Traditionally, you are taking on the risk that the hedger wants to get rid of. Of course, in today's fast paced markets, speculators vie against speculators, and hedgers have a smaller, but still important, role.

It's important to understand that the word "speculator" has a very precise meaning in commodities futures trading, a meaning that is different from the derogatory connotation sometimes given it in other contexts. As a speculator, you are a legitimate investor in a highly evolved and legitimate market place.

There's nothing wrong with being a commodities speculator. The markets are crying for more people to try it. The only thing wrong is going into the market and losing, but of course, that's what this book aims to help you avoid.

APPENDIX 2
THE LINTNER STUDY—AN EVALUATION

If an investor's only goal is to attain the highest achievable return, he would place his funds in an investment vehicle with the greatest expected return. His wealth would be staked to the success or failure of the particular investment. Most investors recognize the great risks inherent in a "putting all your eggs in one basket" strategy. Any change in the present or future economic environment could mean financial disaster.

Investors tend to be risk-adverse and to look to lower their broadside risk by spreading their capital into a variety of investments. The value of investment diversification was first quantified by the work of Harry Markowitz. He established methods to evaluate how mixing investments affected portfolio risk. He demonstrated that the standard deviation of a collection of investments would be lower than the weight average of the standard deviation of the individual securities.

Investments react differently to changes in the economy. Stocks and bonds are positively correlated so they tend to move in the same direction. On the other hand, commodity and financial futures are negatively correlated with the returns of stocks and bonds. Those investments which have low correlation create opportunities for investors seeking to diversify their portfolios.

By using Modern Portfolio Theory techniques of aligning investments of low correlation together, an investor is able to reduce overall portfolio volatility without giving up any expected return. A portfolio of stocks and futures would be less volatile than a portfolio of futures or a portfolio of stocks because their individual returns are negatively correlated. The variability in portfolio returns would fall because when stocks show gains, the value of futures falls and vice versa. The result is a portfolio constructed so that it will perform reasonably well in most economic environments.

RESEARCH

In May 1983, Professor John Lintner of the Harvard Business School presented a paper to the Financial Analysts Federation. Lintner's research, titled "The Potential Role of Managed Commodity-Financial Futures Accounts (And/ Or Funds) in Portfolios of Stock and Bonds" emphasized the benefits of investment diversification. His work showed that by adding investments in managed accounts of trading advisors or publicly traded futures funds to more conventional portfolios of stocks and bonds, an investor could achieve a greater return, often with less risk.

Lintner's research covered a 42-month period from mid-1979 through the end of 1982. The current study was undertaken to test Lintner's theories over a longer time period. An historical period of 69 months from March 1979 through the end of 1984 (encompassing both turbulent and sluggish markets) was analyzed.

SUMMARY OF RISKS AND RETURNS

The "Average Monthly Returns and Risks" is a summary page of the investor performance over the study's time period. Six different investments are evaluated—the Leading Manager Index, the Leading Funds Index, common stocks, corporate bonds, a 60 percent stock and 40 percent bond portfolio, and Treasury bills.

Each investment's average monthly return and standard deviation have been calculated. Through dividing the return by the standard deviation, a return/risk ratio is developed. The largest loss and highest return in any month is included to show the extent of peaks and valleys in the investment's monthly swings. The number of months of gain and loss is also included.

This summary page is broken into three sections. The first part is raw or actual returns. The second section is excess monthly returns. This excess return is the return earned less earnings foregone on a "safe" investment, i.e. Treasury Bills. The third section is real monthly returns. Real returns are raw returns less the inflation rate.

Average Monthly Returns and Risks
3/79–12/84

Portfolio Composition	Avg. Mo. Return	Std. Dev. of Return	Return/ Risk Ratio	Largest Loss Any Month	Highest Return Any Month	# Months Gain or Loss
Raw Returns						
Leading Manager Index	2.108	8.601	.245	−11.74	28.11	34.5/34.5
Leading Funds Index	1.055	6.963	.152	−15.74	21.11	36/33
Common Stock Portfolio	1.238	4.271	.290	−9.71	12.67	44/25
Corporate Bonds	.778	4.539	.171	−8.90	14.19	37/32
60% Stocks & 40% Bonds	1.053	3.665	.287	−7.50	10.75	43/26
Treasury Bills	.870	.206	4.224			

Average Monthly Returns and Risks
3/79–12/84 *(continued)*

Portfolio Composition	Avg. Mo. Return	Std. Dev. of Return	Return/ Risk Ratio	Largest loss any month	Highest Return any month	# months gain or loss
Excess Mo. Returns (less T-Bills)						
Leading Manager Index	1.238	8.609	.144	−12.79	27.31	31/38
Leading Funds Index	.186	6.964	.027	−16.51	20.08	29/40
Common Stock Portfolio	.368	4.339	.085	−10.90	11.91	36/33
Corporate Bonds	−.093	4.524	−.021	−9.78	12.94	33/36
60% Stocks & 40% Bonds	.184	3.705	.050	−8.37	9.83	35/34
Real Mo. Returns (less CPI)						
Leading Manager Index	1.510	8.557	.176	−12.31	26.66	31/38
Leading Funds Index	.457	6.905	.066	−17.03	20.30	31/38
Common Stock Portfolio	.639	4.355	.147	−11.16	12.45	37/32
Corporate Bonds	.178	4.648	.038	−9.79	13.07	35/34
60% Stocks & 40% Bonds	.455	3.777	.120	−8.39	10.53	36/33
Treasury Bills	.272	.387	.703			

RISK/RETURN CURVE

Each point on the Portfolio of Futures and Stocks and Bonds curve (below) represents a different mix of investments. The curve shows the return/risk tradeoff an investor faces in choosing a pool of investments. An investor can choose to achieve higher returns by accepting higher risks or he can choose to minimize his risk and sacrifice a higher return.

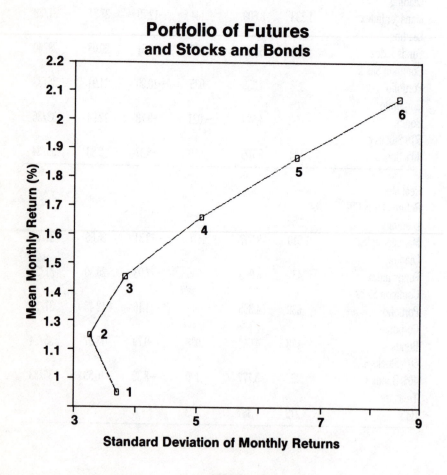

Portfolio of Futures and Stocks and Bonds

Portfolio of Futures and Stocks and Bonds

Graph Point #	Portfolio Composition	Mean Monthly Return	Standard Deviation	Return/Risk Ratio
1	60% Stocks & 40% Bonds	1.053	3.665	.287
2	20% Futures & 80% S & B	1.265	3.196	.396
3	40% Futures & 60% S & B	1.476	3.829	.385
4	60% Futures & 40% S & B	1.686	5.173	.326
5	80% Futures & 20% S & B	1.897	6.822	.278
6	100% Futures	2.108	8.601	.245

An investor selects his position on this curve depending on his willingness to accept risk. An investor will look for the most efficient pool of investments, a portfolio that will maximize his return at a given level of risk.

It becomes obvious that an investor would be much better off following the investment strategy of Portfolio 2 than Portfolio 1. Portfolio 2 is farther to the left (less risk) and higher than Portfolio 1 (higher return) on the return/risk curve. Portfolio 1 represents an investment of 60 percent stock and 40 percent bonds. Portfolio 2 is composed of 20 percent futures and 80 percent stocks and bonds. Over the study's time period, an investor sacrificed not only greater returns, but also lower portfolio volatility by not including futures in his investment pool of stocks and bonds.

The lack of correlation between futures and stocks and bonds smooth out the returns of the portfolio so the monthly change in portfolio value is more steady and consistent.

DATA USED

The Leading Manager Index (LMI) and Leading Funds Index (LFI) as reported in Managed Account Reports were used for the analysis of commodity and financial futures investment performance.

The LMI is an unweighted composite average of the performance of 10 managers trading private pools and individual managed accounts.

The LFI represents the mean performance of 14 publicly offered funds. None of the funds included in the index have trading managers in common; therefore the index is a good representation of the public funds offered today.

Both indices are quality benchmarks for measuring the performance of future funds and private pools as a whole. Recently Managed Account Reports shows that the coefficient of correlation between the indices and the total offerings of the future funds and private pools was over .90, where 1.00 represents perfect positive correlation.

The monthly average reported for the LMI and the LFI is the new net asset value of the index. The base of 100 is January, 1982. The new net asset value is calculated by dividing month-end net asset value (NAV) per unit less any cash distributions by the NAC on January 1. This figure is then multiplied by 100. In the case of the Leading Manager Index, each manager's NAV for each monthly period is totaled with the NAVs of the other nine managers and divided by 10 to create an unweighted composite average. The same procedure would be followed for the LFI, except each fund NAV constructed would be added with the other 13 and divided by 14 to develop the monthly index.

The common stock index used in the study is based upon the Standard & Poor's composite index. Reinvestment of dividends paid during the month occur on the final trading day of each month at the S & P's index's closing price level.

The corporate bond index used was the Salomon Brothers High Grade Long Term Corporate Bond Index. The monthly total returns include coupon reinvestment.

The U.S. Treasury Bill index was created from the Wall Street Journal and the Consumer Price Index from the U.S. Department of Labor, Bureau of Labor Statistics.

ADDING FUTURES TO A
STOCK AND BOND PORTFOLIO

These examples will provide greater statistical evidence to the value of diversifying a portfolio by adding investments in futures.

Adding Futures to a Stock and Bond Portfolio

Portfolio Composition	Avg. Mo. Return	Std. Dev. of Return	Ret./Risk Ratio	Invest 3/1/79	Value 1/1/85	Total Return
60% Stocks & 40% Bonds	1.053	3.665	.287	$1,000	$1,972	97.2%
100% Stocks	1.238	4.271	.290	$1,000	$2,202	120.2%
20% Futures & 48% Stocks & 32% Bonds	1.265	3.196	.396	$1,000	$2,301	130.1%

Adding Futures to a Stock and Bond Portfolio

Portfolio Composition	Avg. Mo. Return	Std. Dev. of Return	Ret./Risk Ratio	Invest 3/1/79	Value 1/1/85	Total Return
60% Stocks & 40% Bonds	1.053	3.665	.287	$1,000	$1,972	97.2%
100% Stocks	1.238	4.271	.290	$1,000	$2,202	120.2%
40% Futures & 30% Stocks & 30% Bonds	1.476	3.829	.385	$1,000	$2,619	161.9%

Adding Futures to a Stock and Bond Portfolio

Portfolio Composition	Avg. Mo. Return	Std. Dev. of Return	Ret./Risk Ratio	Invest 3/1/79	Value 1/1/85	Total Return
100% Stocks	1.238	4.271	.290	$1,000	$2,202	120.2%
40% Futures & 60% Stocks	1.586	3.975	.399	$1,000	$2,815	181.5%

In this example an investor can achieve a 2 percent increase in his monthly return and reduce his portfolio volatility 13 percent by adding futures to investment of stocks and bonds.

Three different portfolios are examined:

1. A portfolio of 60 percent common stocks and 40 percent corporate bonds,
2. A portfolio comprised of common stocks, and
3. A portfolio of 20 percent financial and commodity futures using the Leading Manager Index (LMI) and 48 percent common stocks and 32 percent corporate bonds.

In the first portfolio of 60 percent stocks and 40 percent bonds, an investor would receive a monthly return of 1.053 percent with a standard deviation of 3.665. An investment of $1,000 in 3/1/79 would have grown to $1,972 in 1/1/85. If an investor held a portfolio of 100 percent common stocks over the same time period, his average monthly return would climb to 1.238 percent a month. However, the investor would be faced with more portfolio volatility as there is now less diversity in his pool of investments.

If you compare return/risk ratios between the two portfolios, you discover that the increase in monthly return by holding 100 percent stocks in a portfolio instead of a mix of 60 percent stocks and 40 percent bonds is offset by the rise in standard deviation from 3.665 to 4.271. The return/risk ratios are almost identical: .287 for a portfolio of 60 percent stocks and 40 percent bonds and .290 for a portfolio of 100 percent stocks.

A risk-adverse investor would be much better off to add a 20 percent position in futures to his portfolio of 60 percent stocks and 40 percent bonds. The new portfolio composition would be 20 percent futures, 48 percent stocks, and 32 percent bonds. Although the increase in mean monthly return between a portfolio of stocks and bonds and a portfolio of 20 percent futures and stocks and bonds is modest (only an increase from 1.053 to 1.265), the impact on portfolio risk is quite significant. The standard deviation of a portfolio of 20 percent futures and 48 percent stocks and 32 percent bonds is 3.196. The standard deviations of the other two portfolios are much higher. The reason is the lack of correlation between futures and stocks and bonds.

Over the study time period, the monthly returns of the Leading Manager Index (LMI) used to represent an investment in futures, were found to be uncorrelated with the returns of both common stocks and corporate bonds. The intercorrelations with the LMI and common stocks (−.148) and corporate bonds (−0.61) were actually negative.

The result of this lack of correlation is a portfolio mix of futures, stocks, and bonds that is less volatile. In 34 months of the 69 of the study, the LMI showed an increase in net asset value. The lack of the correlation between the LMI and the stock index can be shown in the number of months the stock index moved in a positive direction with the futures. In the 34 months that the futures showed a net gain, the stock index rose 17 times and fell 17 times. In the same period the bond index rose 18 times and fell 16 times.

In another example an investor can achieve a much larger return with a small increase in portfolio volatility.

In this example, if an investor increases his position to 40 percent futures and 60 percent stocks and bonds, the portfolio's monthly return jumps to 1.476 percent. The standard deviation of 3.8929 is still less than the standard deviation of a portfolio consisting solely of stocks (4.271) and is slightly larger than a portfolio of 60 percent stocks and 40 percent bonds (3.665). The return/risk ratio of .385 for the portfolio including futures is 33 percent greater than a portfolio of 100 percent stocks and 34 percent larger than a portfolio of 60 percent stocks and 40 percent bonds.

The investment composed of 40 percent futures reaches a value of $2,619 by the start of the last year of the study, 19 percent more than the value of a 100 percent stock portfolio and 32 percent greater than a portfolio of 60 percent stocks and 40 percent bonds.

ADDING FUTURES TO A STOCK PORTFOLIO

In a portfolio of stocks and bonds, it was shown that by replacing 20 percent of the portfolio value with investment in futures, an investor could achieve a higher return with lower risk. If he increased the investment in futures to 40 percent of total portfolio value, the return climbed, but portfolio volatility was greater.

In an all-stock portfolio, a greater percentage of investments in futures can be made with the positive effects of efficient diversification driving up return and decreasing the portfolio risk.

In this example, the all-stock portfolio has as monthly mean return of 1.238 percent and a standard deviation of

4.271. If an investor placed $1,000 in an all-stock portfolio, his investment would have grown to $2,202 over the 69-month period.

The results are quite significant if an investor replaces 40 percent of the stock in his portfolio with investments in futures. The new portfolio of 40 percent futures and 60 percent stocks is 7.5 percent less volatile as the standard deviation falls to 3.975. The mean monthly return climbs 28 percent from 1.238 percent to 1.586 percent. The investor enjoys a total return of 181.5 percent on the mixed portfolio as the account value jumps from $1,000 at the beginning of the study period to $2,815 at the end.

One method of measuring if the high returns of futures investments are worth accepting additional risks is to compare the return/risk ratios on the chart on pages 206–207. Reward/risk ratios of futures investments (LMI & LFI) are compared with the ratio for portfolios of stocks, bonds, and a mix of stocks and bonds. The ratio comparison is made at three levels: raw or actual returns, excess returns (returns less earnings on Treasury Bills—these being considered a safe investment), and real returns (the return of an investment after inflation is taken into account).

The average fund manager has not provided a return/risk ratio worth taking the risk during the time period studied. In the shortened time period of Lintner's work, funds had returns close to those of managed accounts, but performance has since fallen. Because of the poor performance of funds, the analysis has been limited to studying the Leading Manager Index.

When comparing the return/risk ratios using actual returns, the ratio for the ten managers that make up the Leading Manager Index was about 80 percent of that for

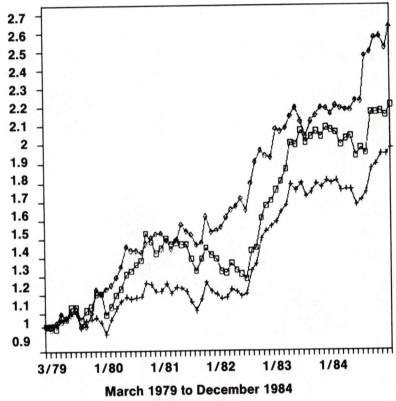

Portfolio Returns Based On
Diversifying Stocks, Bonds, and Futures

March 1979 to December 1984

100% Stocks - □   **+ 60% S & 40% B**   **△ 20% FUT & 80% S & B**

Portfolio returns based on diversifying: 100 percent stocks; 60 percent stocks and 40 percent bonds; and 40 percent futures and 60 percent stocks and bonds.

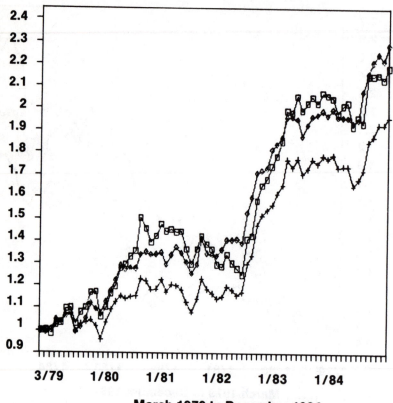

Portfolio Returns Based On
Diversifying Stocks, Bonds, and Futures

March 1979 to December 1984

100% Stocks - □   **+ 60% S & 40% B**   △ **40% FUT & 60% S & B**

Portfolio returns based on diversifying: 100 percent stocks; 60 percent stocks and 40 percent bonds; and 20 percent futures and 80 percent stocks and bonds.

stock and 90 percent for a portfolio of stocks and bonds. The ratio comparison shows a much more favorable result when you allow for T-bill earnings and the inflation rate. The average manager in the LMI earned a return/risk ratio almost three times as large as a portfolio of stocks and bonds when monthly returns for T-bills were taken away. The average manager provided a ratio about twice as great as a portfolio of stocks. When considering the return/risk ratio after adjustments for inflation, the average manager provided a ratio one and a half times as large as a stock and bond portfolio, and a ratio 1.2 times greater than a portfolio of stocks.

Reward/Risk Ratios

Actual Monthly Returns	u/o	Ratio Avg. to Stocks	Ratio Avg. to Bonds	Ratio Avg. to S & B
Leading Manager Index	.245	.845	1.433	.854
Leading Funds Index	.152	.524	.889	.530
Common Stock Portfolio	.290			
Corporate Bond Portfolio	.171			
60/40 Stocks & Bonds Portfolio	.287			
Excess Returns (less T-bills)				

Reward/Risk Ratios *(continued)*

Actual Monthly Returns	u/o	Ratio Avg. to Stocks	Ratio Avg. to Bonds	Ratio Avg. to S & B
Leading Manager Index	.144	1.694	**	2.880
Leading Funds Index	.027	.318	**	.540
Common Stock Portfolio	.085			
Corporate Bond Portfolio	-0.21			
60/40 Stocks & Bonds Portfolio	.050			
Real Returns (less CPI)				
Leading Manager Index	.176	1.197	**	1.467
Leading Funds Index	.066	.449	**	.564
Common Stock Portfolio	.147			
Corporate Bond Portfolio	.038			
60/40 Stocks & Bonds Portfolio	.120			

Lintner wrote in his study that, "The period July 1979–December 1982 may not be a fully adequate basis for forming numerical assessments of the future levels of returns and risks." He believed that the general findings of his work—that low correlations exist between investments in futures and portfolios of stocks and bonds— would not change much in the future.

Using the expanded period of this study, the intercorrelations between futures and stocks and bonds were found to be statistically insignificant, and in many cases negative correlation existed. This lack of correlation between managed futures funds and public futures account funds strengthens the point that adding futures to an existing stock or mixed stock and bond portfolio will be beneficial to the diversification aims of investors. Through this diversification, the risks involved in attaining a return are reduced which leads to an improved return/risk ratio.

PORTFOLIO COMPOSITION

To aid in the evaluation of mixing investments, a variety of portfolios were constructed. Portfolios composed of the Leading Manager Index (LMI) and Leading Funds Index (LFI) (used to represent the performance of financial and commodity futures investments) were added to portfolios of common stocks and corporate bonds. The percentage each asset makes up in the portfolio varies from 20 percent to 80 percent.

The table shows the performance (average monthly return), the risk (standard deviation), the return/risk ratio, the largest monthly gain or loss over the time period studied, and the number of months the portfolio had a gain or loss in value.

Reward/Risk Ratios (u/o) and Intercorrelations

Actual Monthly Returns	u/o	LMI	LFI	Stock	Bond	S&B
Leading Manager Index	.245	1.000				
Leading Funds Index	.152	.689	1.000			
Common Stock Portfolio	.290	−.148	−.023			
Corporate Bonds	.171	−.061	.028	.383	1.000	
60/40 Stocks & Bonds Portfolio	.287	−.133	−.002	.889	.763	1.000
Excess Returns (less T-bills)						
Leading Manager Index	.144	1.000				
Leading Funds Index	.027	.690	1.000			
Common Stock Portfolio	.085	.267	−0.13	1.000		
Corporate Bonds	−.021	−.061	.026	.390	1.000	
60/40 Stocks & Bonds Portfolio	.050	−.125	.004	.893	.762	1.000
Real Returns (less CPI)						
Leading Manager Index	.176	1.000				
Leading Funds Index	.066	.686	1.000			
Common Stock Portfolio	.147	−.146	−.024	1.000		
Corporate Bonds	.038	−.056	.031	.410	1.000	
60/40 Stocks & Bonds Portfolio	.120	−.129	.001	.894	.776	1.000

Average Monthly Returns and Risks, Portfolio Mixes Including Futures

Portfolio Composition	Avg. Mo. Return	Std. Dev. of Return	Return/ Risk Ratio	Largest Loss Any Month	Highest Return Any Month	# Months Gain or Loss
20% LMI & 80% Stock	1.412	3.592	.393	−7.08	11.49	48/21
40% LMI & 60% Stock	1.586	3.975	.399	−7.60	14.91	44.5/24.5
60% LMI & 40% Stock	1.760	5.192	.339	−8.13	19.31	41/27
80% LMI & 20% Stock	1.934	6.808	.284	−9.82	23.71	36/33
20% LFI & 80% Stock	1.202	3.660	.328	−8.52	10.93	47.5/21.5
40% LFI & 60% Stock	1.165	3.741	.311	−7.33	9.18	41/28
60% LFI & 40% Stock	1.129	4.477	.252	−9.01	11.17	39/30
80% LFI & 20% Stock	1.092	5.615	.194	−12.37	16.01	36/33
20% LMI & 80% Bonds	1.043	3.923	.266	−8.96	13.10	40/29
40% LMI & 60% Bonds	1.310	4.256	.308	−9.01	14.28	37/32
60% LMI & 40% Bonds	1.576	5.366	.294	−9.06	17.28	37/32
80% LMI & 20% Bonds	1.842	6.886	.267	−9.32	21.14	34/35
20% LFI & 80% Bonds	.830	3.927	.211	−8.37	12.50	37/32
40% LFI & 60% Bonds	.889	3.950	.225	−7.84	11.85	33/36

Average Monthly Returns and Risks, Portfolio Mixes Including Futures (continued)

Portfolio Composition	Avg. Mo. Return	Std. Dev. of Return	Return/ Risk Ratio	Largest Loss Any Month	Highest Return Any Month	# Months Gain or Loss
60% LFI & 40% Bonds	.944	4.602	.205	−9.57	12.07	34/35
80% LFI & 20% Bonds	1.000	5.669	.176	−12.65	16.59	34/35
20% LMI & 80% S & B	1.265	3.196	.396	−7.83	9.96	45/24
40% LMI & 60% S & B	1.476	3.829	.385	−8.17	11.82	43.5/25.5
60% LMI & 40% S & B	1.686	5.173	.326	−8.50	17.25	38/21
80% LMI & 20% S & B	1.897	6.822	.278	−9.13	22.68	36/33
20% LFI & 80% S & B	1.054	3.242	.325	−7.24	9.39	42.5/26.5
40% LFI & 60% S & B	1.055	3.545	.298	−6.99	8.70	39/30
60% LFI & 40% S & B	1.055	4.424	.238	−9.23	11.37	38/31
80% LFI & 20% S & B	1.056	5.617	.188	−12.49	16.24	34/35

By reviewing the mixes of investment vehicles in a portfolio, an investor can study the return/risk tradeoffs and make a decision on the return he desires or the amount of risk he is willing to accept. For example, an investor can adjust the percentage of futures (LMI) held in his portfolio to increase the return to the point where he reaches the maximum level of risk he is willing to accept.

CONCLUSION

This study confirms Lintner's earlier observations that the low correlations, even negative correlations in many cases, between returns on investment in futures and investments in stocks or bonds make futures an excellent addition to a portfolio.

Not only were portfolio volatility reduced and better return/risk tradeoffs created, but in some cases greater overall returns were achieved. In particular, an account composed of 60 percent common stocks and 40 percent corporate bonds was greatly enhanced by the addition of an investment in futures. Creating a portfolio where futures compose 20 percent of its value and stocks and bonds the remaining 80 percent increased the monthly return and lowered portfolio risk over a portfolio of 60 percent stocks and 40 percent bonds. An investor enjoyed similar results if he diversified from a 100 percent stock portfolio to a portfolio of 40 percent futures and 60 percent stocks.

INDEX